D1518372

THE BLIND MAN TRACES THE CIRCLE

THE BLIND MAN
TRACES THE CIRCLE

On the Patterns
and Philosophy of
Byron's Poetry

BY M. G. COOKE

PRINCETON, NEW JERSEY
PRINCETON UNIVERSITY PRESS
1969

Printed in the United States of America
by Princeton University Press

This book has been composed in Linotype Caledonia.

TO NELLA RUBENS

PREFACE

There have been times, in the peculiar evolution of Byron studies, when critics have made it appear somehow unseemly to praise Byron as a poet unless such praise came parceled up with some pointed strictures. Since Lockhart's "John Bull's Letter to the Right Honorable Lord Byron" remained for many years singular in its double-edged views, Swinburne may be cited as the one who with his essay on Byron initiated the trend of ambivalent opinion. He is also the one who, taking back whatever good he had had to say, initially identified that ambivalence when in a second essay, on Wordsworth and Byron, he took such elegantly fierce exception to the way Arnold's piece on Byron had "now and then spread a wider sail before a stronger wind of sheer paradox than ever has any critic of anything like equal . . . reputation."

The paradox clearly lies in Arnold's tactic of asking the reader to honor a "splendid" and "true and puissant personality" in Byron while observing that the expression of this personality betrays a lack of reflective power, an uncouth sentimentality, and an uncertain style. After Arnold, Paul Elmer More and T. S. Eliot have also memorably taken a half-adverse view of Byron. More proves hardly less compelling in his portrayal of Byron's loud descents into the ludicrous and his "want of discipline" (Arnold had said "self-discipline") than he is in arguing the wholesomeness of the Byronic revival. And Eliot, if he does not quite make "frankness," "abundance," and "raffish honesty" into patronized virtues, largely obliterates the effects of his salute with his pronouncements

on Byron's commonplace writing and thinking, and devotion of "gigantic energy" to a "petty purpose."

Yet few at the worst of times have followed the dis-
affected Swinburne—who well may have used the romantic poet as a stalking-horse to invade Arnold's critical demesne—in ranking Byron as a "poet of the third
class who now and then rises into the second." At least
few have treated him as such. As Arnold remarked,
though the heyday of Byron's reputation had passed,
"his name [was] still great and brilliant." It has remained throughout a name of considerable account.
Paradoxically perhaps, Byron instead of ever dropping
back into the flickering valley of minor poets, seems to
have taken on the status of a "bad" major poet.

How far such an estimation bespeaks a partial reading
in the light of some autocratic set of expectations
(Arnold's requirement of a criticism of life, More's pro-
classical principles, Eliot's insistence on verbal inventive-
ness and élan) it would be difficult to tell. It does seem
clear, though, that as long as Byron was being apologized
for as a poet, his poetry was studied much less minutely,
much less zestfully than his life with its tangle of
passions and crises, its glory and distress, its mélange
of magnanimity and decadence. We can now appreciate
the fact that what was needed to settle the biographical
spate was a comprehensive biography, or, to put first
things first, a comprehending biographer. Leslie A.
Marchand's 3-volume *Byron: A Biography* appeared a
decade ago, and was found to be at home with the co-
pious and complex details of Byron's life, sober and yet
authoritative in statement, penetrating and balanced in
judgment. Since then, as seeming by-products, biographical study has continued not so much on as around

Byron, while strictly critical work on him has grown appreciably in volume and in discriminating independence. Not that any letter-perfect line of demarcation offers itself; Frye and Davie are still treating Byron with condescending acknowledgement, and Gerard, Calvert, Knight, and Lovell responded to him with serious and discerning criticism during the biographical state. A reformed emphasis is as much as can be claimed, but truly that seems enough.

In general, dissection of the Byronic ego, in the manner of Praz or Vulliamy or du Bos, gives way to a wider recognition of the active and original qualities of Byron's thought and style in Ridenour, Lovell and Marchand (once again), Rutherford, Bostetter, Kernan, Pratt, Steffan, Thorslev, Joseph, Pafford, and Marshall. Even more auspiciously, Karl Kroeber in his study of *Romantic Narrative Art* has, without a trace of apology or special pleading, put Byron forward as a seminally romantic poet. It may be that Byron has the advantage of the fact that as our conception of romanticism grows larger, and at the same time more particular, it includes him with less disturbance, and makes our conception of him at once larger and more particular.

At this stage, we need to face the peculiar liability of current Byron criticism to take one of two forms: the monograph, and what is in effect the miscellany. This criticism scrutinizes one work (say, *Don Juan*), one topic or theme (e.g., Byron's view of nature and specifically of mountain or sea, his portrayal of the hero, or his exploitation of the eighteenth-century novel), one formal concern (such as structure); or else it ranges at large over Byron's work, taking it as an apodictically heterogeneous mass, and displaying a certain abruptness of passage from one work or class of works to another. Both approaches, the specialized and the versatile, have their advantages, and both have been used with distinction. Another approach also calls out for use, the synthesizing approach, which has perhaps been foreshadowed by Bostetter, with his perception of a vital link between *Manfred* and *Don Juan* (though he does not go on to take the wholly consistent step of connecting *Don Juan* and *The Deformed Transformed* or *The Island*). Robert F. Gleckner's study of *Byron and the Ruins of Paradise* must also be cited here; it argues eloquently against the miscellaneous or anthologist's approach and treats the Byron corpus without stinting. But it, too, differs from the synthesis that is to be sought, constituting a sort of amplified monograph, a topology of perennial gloom in Byron's work.

The synthesizing approach immediately differs from the monograph in scope and from the miscellany in centrality of concern. It differs, too, from the tack taken by Francis Jeffrey of homogenizing Byron's work by seeing "voluptuousness" everywhere on its surface and "misanthropy" everywhere at its core. Basically it expresses the sense that Byron's poems transcend a collection and exist as a body of poetry, with a consistent and plausible articulation. The present study advances such a reading of the Byron corpus, attempting to follow the pattern of its development not because that appears abstractly desirable, but because it has projected itself as concretely necessary and sound.

This is not meant to sound any bugling *beot* regarding originality for the work; its points of contact with prior criticism have been, even where agreement fails, too valuable for that, and besides it has had originality less than responsibility in view. Still, it should not come amiss to point to certain methodological gains, such as recognition of the kinship in philosophy between *The Two Foscari* and *Don Juan*; of the common stylistic features of *Childe Harold, Mazeppa,* and *Don Juan*; of the related concerns underlying *The Age of Bronze, The Deformed Transformed,* and *The Island*; and finally of the reflection in the final lyrics of the early ones.

In terms of emphases and perspectives, too, certain new departures will be evident. Byron's lyrics get more space, more serious scrutiny than heretofore, and justifiably so. Many of them prove not just comely as lyrics, but crucial as indices of the authenticity and richness of the author's place in the romantic complex, to say nothing of their revising our evaluation of his contact with Wordsworthian naturalism in 1816. The problem of coherence in such diverse works as *The Giaour, Childe Harold* III, and *Don Juan* is taken up afresh, with regard to the issues—both aesthetic and conceptual— that are involved and to the configurations of structure and style which inhibit Byron or set him winging as he writes. The problem of his indecorum, especially at the culmination of the Siege of Ismail, comes in for unindignant and overdue reassessment. The view of the overvaulting will or, alternatively, of tenacious reason as a good or a promise of good in a problematical universe, in short the syndrome of "Promethean" posturing in pieces like *Manfred* and *Cain* and *Childe Harold* III and IV, is examined for possible morbidity; this is put with recent understanding of such poems as "The Prisoner of Chillon" and the "Ode to Napoleon Buonaparte" to suggest an overall conception of Byron's treatment of will.

Byron's ever more purposive and skillful manipulations of imagery and structure to convey epistemological insights get ampler consideration, and his unique relation to his audience in a peculiarly inward-oriented period gets a closer inspection than in the past. Above all, in addition to locating the point of existential upheaval before the eruptions of 1815-1816, the study offers evidence of an actual recovery of poise taking place around 1821 and continuing, though not unshakably, to the end of his life. The seemingly spontaneous affirmations of the early lyrics thus find their counterpart in the more deliberate affirmations of *The Two Foscari* and *Don Juan* and other late writings.

The study is arranged, by a selection and combination of particular perspectives, to frame an integral, unambiguous image of Byron's poetry and of his mind. The result has been what could seem, for a fairly substantial enterprise, a fairly concise text. But surely that is all to the good? Shortcomings would appear to boil down to a question of concinnity rather than of conciseness in the work, which is inevitably still for the interested writer an "object over near." With due recognition, then, of what impartial time and criticism may show up, it should suffice to say that this study, weaving together careful criticism in neglected areas of Byron's work, untapped possibilities of response to perennial problems, and enlarged contexts for setting off old conclusions, has sought in effect to throw a single net over the apparent Proteus of the romantic period.

ACKNOWLEDGMENTS

Critics and scholars perhaps pursue a lonelier career than most in these corporate days, but few since Aristotle have been denied the benefit of working with instructors and colleagues. Thus, in keeping with the laws of candor no less than the impulses of gratitude, I would like to note the chief among the persons who have moved me with advice, assistance, and inspiration along the way to the present publication. Professor Martin Price of Yale University, some years ago, started me thinking carefully about Byron and aspiring to say something material about his work. Not long thereafter I found myself trying my wings on a Byron dissertation at the University of California at Berkeley, under the generous if also demanding tutelage of Professors James R. Caldwell and Josephine Miles. That venture has yielded, besides a high degree of invaluable training, a brief article on "The Restoration Ethos of Byron's Classical Plays" and a handful of pages in the present study which have been recast and put forward in line with revised and, one is obliged to presume, rectified estimates of Byron's mind and work. I trust that Professor Price will not have cause to shake his head at what he started, and hope that Professor Miles will see something closer here to what she and Professor Caldwell (since regrettably deceased) urged me to imagine might be done. But let me, having given this background, also ask that the sins of my generation not be visited upon those who have encouraged me and my work.

I have in more recent times enjoyed searching, inspiriting conversation with Professor Harold Bloom of Yale University and Professor Robert F. Gleckner of the

University of California at Riverside, both of whom read the study at different stages of progress. Further notable encouragement was offered me by Professor Richard S. Sylvester of Yale University. I would also voice special thanks to Professors Robert J. Griffin and A. Bartlett Giamatti of Yale University for nameless but neither little nor unremembered acts of thoughtfulness and interest.

A portion of the time that I was fortunate enough to have free on a Morse Fellowship from Yale University was devoted to the final preparation of the study, and completion would have been appreciably delayed but for the very considerate and efficient help of Miss Ann Lincoln, Executive Secretary, and Mrs. Doris Pfuderer, Secretary, in the English Department at Yale.

John Murray (Publishers) Ltd. have kindly permitted me to make use of *The Works of Lord Byron*, ed. R. E. Prothero and E. H. Coleridge, and also of *The Poetical Works of Lord Byron*, ed. E. H. Coleridge. Quotations from Byron's poetry in my text are drawn from the latter edition.

The greater part of Chapter VI first appeared in the *Keats-Shelley Journal*, Vol. 17 (1968) and is reprinted with the kind permission of the Board of Directors of The Keats-Shelley Association of America, Inc.

The dedication is an earnest of my final, and first debt.

CONTENTS

ABBREVIATIONS

CH   *Childe Harold's Pilgrimage*, referred to in the body of the text by the short title *Childe Harold*.

DJ   *Don Juan*.

LJ   *The Works of Lord Byron. Letters and Journals*, ed. Rowland E. Prothero. 6 vols. London, 1898-1901.

PW   *The Works of Lord Byron. Poetry*, ed. Ernest Hartley Coleridge. 7 vols. London, 1898-1905.

THE BLIND MAN TRACES THE CIRCLE

The circle—figure of perfection.

Given the radical asymmetry of the human figure, the blind man cannot unaided go in a straight line, but roughly traces a circle.

· I ·

BYRON AND THE
ROMANTIC LYRIC

*Rebellion itself will often turn out to be the
upsurge of a profound struggle to learn and to
belong.* AUTHOR UNKNOWN

With his statement that a poet must create the taste by
which he is enjoyed, Wordsworth may be taken to have
signalized a tension, perhaps an implicit severance, in
the relation between poet and audience. This sort of tension doubtless marks the history of satirical poetry,
especially where irony ranks high among its features.
That is in the nature of the type. But where that tension
stands out in lyrical or philosophical poetry it becomes
uneasy and problematical, with injured and defiant poets
facing an injured and defiant audience—the posture, in
literature, that is tantamount to revolution.[1]

---

[1] Ostensibly, Wordsworth is arguing in the *Essay Supplementary
to the Preface* of 1815 that throughout English literary history
the poet, "as far as he is great and at the same time *original*, has
had the task of *creating* the taste by which he is to be enjoyed:
so has it been, so will it continue to be." At times, however, he
appears to be dealing with the "strange . . . obliquities of admiration" rather than with the problem or process of creating taste;
and he is willing to concede 1) that "the predecessors of an original Genius of a high order will have smoothed the way for . . .
much [that] he will have in common" with them, and 2) that "in
the works of every true poet [there] will be found passages of
that species of excellence, which is proved by effects immediate
and universal." In actuality Wordsworth, not without a tinge of
self-contradiction, is both generalizing his views on the tardiness
of taste to cover all ages, and significantly qualifying those views.
The idea of a romantic revolution may be seen to hold good in
any case. For Wordsworth, through his "philosophical Friend," has
raised the accidental phenomenon of delayed reputation into a

The romantic revolution, it is generally acknowledged,
had among its chief features a new flourishing of lyric
poetry, pertaining not just to degrees of excellence, but
actually to the nature of the lyric. For even though "the
lyric poets of the sixteenth century were less personal
than the great Romantics,"[2] lyric poetry now began to
carry philosophy as more than a secondary freight assumed from, and shaped in, the realm of prose.[3] It elected
to move outside of, or to redefine what Hazlitt in *The
Spirit of the Age* comfortably called "the circle of nature
and received opinion." In effect the lyric, without the

necessary concept, a law of literature. The novelty and formality
of the concept, not the novelty or inevitability of the phenomenon,
institutes the revolutionary situation.

[2] Kenneth Muir, intro. to his edn. of *Elizabethan Lyrics*, New
York, 1953, p. 24.

[3] "The greatest of the [Elizabethan] sonneteers," says Muir,
"was Shakespeare; but it is important to emphasize that his sonnets depend for part of their effect on the tradition in which they
were written, on the consummate expression of the great com-
monplaces, on the subtle deviations from the conventional . . ."
(p. 27). I suggest that the same goes for all lyrical poetry, when it
embodies anything like articulate philosophy, up to the romantic
period. Donne, with his forceful individuality, is only seemingly an
exception: to read his lyrics without reference to the Elizabethan
World Picture is to do them some injustice. It is, as Basil Willey
points out, in the romantic period that "the modern situation"
originates "the situation in which beliefs are made out of poetry
rather than poetry out of beliefs" (*The Seventeenth Century
Background*, New York, 1950, p. 298). Leone Vivante presents a
forceful summary of the traditional situation in his study of
*English Poetry and its Contribution to the Knowledge of a Crea-
tive Principle*: "It is through the use of words, by eliciting from
them, or recalling them to, a deeper spiritual meaning, that systematic philosophy has been a most vital factor in poetry. Thus
the Italian poets of the fourteenth century—when philosophy
. . . had comparatively a greater part in general culture than it
has today—found at their disposal a glowing *medium* of words,
inherited from ancient philosophy and interpreted, enriched, and
in many respects deepened by medieval philosophers, theologians,
and mystics," New York, 1950, p. 123.

least sacrifice of its ancient subjectivity, sought to expound its own philosophy: of art, for example, of nature, of the mind, and ultimately of being. As Browning would put it, "to know rather consists in opening out a way whence the imprisoned splendour may escape, than in effecting entrance for a light supposed to be without." The sincere romantics lived up to the duty which Remy de Gourmont identifies with sincere men: "ériger en lois ses impressions personnelles."

Wordsworth thus sees the poet as "a man pleased with his own passions and volitions . . . ; delighting to contemplate similar volitions and passions as manifested in the goings-on of the universe, and *habitually impelled to create them* where he does not find them" (italics added). At the same time as he insists that "all good poetry is the spontaneous overflow of powerful feelings," he terms poetry "the first and last of all knowledge" and declares that the object of poetry "is truth, not individual and local, but general, and operative; *not standing upon external testimony,* but carried alive into the heart by passion; truth which is its own testimony, which gives competence and confidence to the tribunal to which it appeals, and receives them from the same tribunal" (italics added).[4] Coleridge likewise asserts the continuum between private experience and general propositions. In a letter of 17 December 1796 to John Thelwall he states: "My philosophical opinions are blended with, or deduced from, my feelings."[5] Shelley writes in the preface to *The Revolt of Islam*: "It is the business of the Poet to

---

[4] The preceding quotations, from the *Preface to Lyrical Ballads,* are taken from *Wordsworth's Literary Criticism,* ed. N. C. Smith, London, 1925.
[5] Quoted from the *Collected Letters of Samuel Taylor Coleridge,* 4 vols., ed. Earl Leslie Griggs, Oxford 1956-59, I, 279.

communicate to others the pleasure and enthusiasm arising out of those images and feelings in the vivid presence of which within his own mind consists at once his inspiration and his reward." The philosophical importance of those "images and feelings" becomes manifest in *A Defence of Poetry*: "A poem is the very image of life expressed in its eternal truth . . . [,] the creation of actions according to the unchangeable forms of human nature, as existing in the mind of the Creator."[6] Keats, too, notwithstanding his distinctions between "Men of Genius" and "Men of Power," and his hopeful pursuit of *Negative Capability*, expresses kindred views in a much-quoted letter to Benjamin Bailey: "I am certain of nothing but of the holiness of the Heart's affections and the truth of Imagination—What the imagination seizes as Beauty must be truth—whether it existed before or not. . . . The Imagination may be compared to Adam's dream —he awoke and found it truth."[7]

The realization of a new philosophical style or, to put it more cautiously, "the attempt to absorb 'truth' into the texture of the lyric"[8] has emerged in recent criticism as a fairly complex process. But even if it took its rise in part from subordinate structures of eighteenth-century literature,[9] with the result that authoritative critics like

[6] *Peacock's Four Ages of Poetry* . . . (Percy Reprints No. 3), ed. H.F.B. Brett-Smith, Oxford, 1953, p. 56.

[7] Quoted from *The Letters of John Keats*, ed. Hyder Edward Rollins, Cambridge, Mass., Vol. i, 1958, 184-185.

[8] Geoffrey H. Hartman, "Wordsworth, Inscriptions, and Romantic Nature Poetry," in *From Sensibility to Romanticism*, ed. Frederick W. Hilles and Harold Bloom, New York, 1965, p. 407.

[9] This question of a developed soil for the growth of romanticism —something Wordsworth tacitly recognizes—has long been canvassed by scholars such as Henry A. Beers (*A History of English Romanticism in the Eighteenth Century*, New York, 1899), but received what may be termed its pivotal presentation in Robert

Hartman find "the real iconoclasts . . . in the period of 1750-1850" ("Wordsworth, Inscriptions," p. 405), there remains good reason to hold that it leapt both off and *away from* the past, so to speak kicking over its platform. Thus M. H. Abrams, while freely calling attention to reminiscent features of the greater romantic lyric, stresses that it is a new lyric form, a romantic invention; indeed he shows Coleridge legitimately and inevitably repudiating Bowles who, probably owing to an overflow of Coleridge's own imaginative energy, had seemed to offer what he was far from possessing.[10] Again Hartman praises "Wordsworth's greatness in recovering elemental situations," but adds:

> It is no part of that greatness to oblige us to recognize the specific prototype or genre. On the contrary, because Wordsworth recovers the generic factor we no longer need to recognize the genre which specialized it. Wordsworth's form appears to be self-generated rather than prompted by tradition, and the greater the poem the clearer this effect.
> ("Wordsworth, Inscriptions," p. 402)

In short, without oversimplifying romanticism as a sourceless phenomenon, the best judgment recognizes "Romantic *freedoms won*" from "the embarrassments of poetic tradition."[11]

Mayo's article, "The Contemporaneity of the Lyrical Ballads," *PMLA*, LXIX (1954), 486-522.

[10] "Structure and Style in the Greater Romantic Lyric," in *From Sensibility to Romanticism*, pp. 527-560, passim.

[11] Harold Bloom, "Keats and the Embarrassments of Poetic Tradition," in *From Sensibility to Romanticism*, p. 225. In dealing here with the embarrassments of poetic tradition, Bloom is avowedly developing on an idea of W. J. Bate in his *John Keats*.

THE BLIND MAN TRACES THE CIRCLE

The romantic lyric itself shows two reasonably distinct styles, to wit: the *exoteric style*, exemplified in the great odes and what Abrams calls greater lyrics, with their overt confrontation of philosophical issues, substantial size, complex form and music, and phrasal intensity and beauty; and the *elemental style* (which we have only recently come to appreciate at its intrinsic value), simple in language and form, ostensibly slight in content as in size, but ultimately presupposing and exercising the values of the more elaborate type. In the latter case a lyric that is *not* "on a conventional theme achieves a concentration" capable of expanding it "into a miniature epic."[12]

This description of the romantic lyric,[13] like many another generalization concerning romantic poetry, would appear to have its Achilles heel in Byron, who is on the whole understood to have failed to write good lyrics, let alone romantic ones. And indeed, not a few

[12] Northrop Frye, *Anatomy of Criticism*, Princeton, 1957, p. 324.

[13] It is practically also a conception of romanticism; romantic poetry tends to operate between, or, more justly, simultaneously *at*, the poles of lyric and philosophy. The great philosophical poem of the period, Wordsworth's *The Prelude*, modifies the epic tradition in a lyrical direction and stands as the lyrical epic. As Harold Bloom puts it in *The Visionary Company*: "we say of Blake and Wordsworth that they are the greatest of the Romantic poets, and indeed the first poets fully to enter into the abyss of their own selves, and we mean that they [thereby] perform for us the work of the ideal metaphysician" (p. 3). The same basic point is made, for example, by Morse Peckham who defines the world of romanticism as one in which "order and value [philosophy] emerge from the perception of the self" ("Toward a Theory of Romanticism: II. Reconsiderations," *SiR.* 1 [Autumn, 1961], 5), and by Herbert Lindenberger in his recognition of "the lyrical impulse" and the "attempt to propound and vividly present a new world-view" as equally characteristic of the romantic age (*On Wordsworth's Prelude*, Princeton, New Jersey, 1963, p. 116).

of his lyrics turn out to be posies tossed off "To a Lady (Who . . .)." Quite a few more may be put down as ersatz cavalier: "To Lesbia" or "To Eliza" or "Reply to Some Verses of J. M. B. Pigot" or "Love's last Adieu" or "Lines Addressed to a Young Lady (Doubtless, sweet girl)." Yet others ("Remember Thee! Remember Thee!" and "A Sketch," for example) strike one as excessively fretful, if not merely visceral, while on the other hand one finds lyrics ("Bright Be the Place of Thy Soul," "If That High World") that partake of an ancient orthodoxy. Byron's sonnets are few, and at best relatively frail. His handful of odes tends to be mired in the topical and personal. The well-turned final lyrics, as Harold Bloom neatly phrases it, "have the poignancy of their occasion."[14] This is something, of course, but not enough. We find much more, if still not enough, in the uncanny beauty of "Stanzas for Music (There be none of Beauty's daughters)" and in the "Stanzas to the Po" with its resignedly passionate resolution. "So We'll Go No More A'Roving," gem though it is, falls short philosophically in not ascending, from the dialectical opposition between time and love, between loving and not being loved, to a higher point of synthesis or reconciliation. If anything, the speaker confesses a sort of psycho-physical attrition which implicitly precludes the achievement of a synthesis either by dint of thought or by bold action. He is not resting for a new adventure; rather he is resting from love, and with full consciousness that its time goes fast and does not return. Presumably the other party to the affair would make the most of whatever time remains to them, but the speaker burkes the notion in an all but formal reversal of the *carpe diem* theme: though the

14 *The Visionary Company*, New York, 1963, p. 292.

heart and the moon still favor love, he (and therefore they) will go no more a'roving. Where at first he may seem just healthily tired from the act of roving, with a tension implied between his purposes and his powers, he proves at last to be essentially, morbidly exhausted. And so the poem, for all its facade of dualistic awareness and logical movement (so, though, for, though, yet) resolves itself into a picture of a state of defeat rather than reaching to a position of affirmation, or even maintaining one of confrontation.

A substantial proportion of Byron's lyrical output will not at first blush rate the romantic cachet; and no one will expect to discover, in his unmethodical writing in prose, any principle to rectify this view, to "create taste." Perhaps the lyrics not summarily eliminated seem as obviously out of harmony with the romantic type. But many of them, though judged to be "of relatively superficial character and value,"[15] will reward the kind of ungrudging scrutiny that has discovered the power of an "elemental" lyric by Blake or Wordsworth.[16] They are

[15] Ward Pafford, "Byron and the Mind of Man: *Childe Harold* III-IV and *Manfred*," *SiR*, I (Winter, 1962), 105. A comparable opinion seems to underlie the brief remarks of Northrop Frye who, while expressing lukewarm praise of the rhythm of some of Byron's lyrics, deprecates the flat diction and conventionality of the lyrics as a whole (*Fables of Identity: Studies in Poetic Mythology*, New York, 1963, pp. 174ff.). The "faint praise" of Byron's lyrical rhythms goes back at least to H.J.C. Grierson, *The Background of English Literature*, London, 1925, pp. 84-85, and *Lyrical Poetry from Blake to Hardy*, London, 1928, p. 45, and is discernible as an undertone in George Saintsbury's *A History of English Prosody*, New York, 1961, III, 95-102. For frank dispraise of Byron's "harmony," one should consult Swinburne's essay, "Wordsworth and Byron" (*The Complete Works*, ed. Edmund Gosse and T. J. Wise, London, 1926, XIV, 162).

[16] Though not concerned with Byron's lyrics as such, George M. Ridenour illustrates the kind of scrutiny I mean in his discussion

romantic lyrics and frequently commendable ones as well. In a typical romantic way they can be shown to encase in a plain, cryptic exterior finely wrought personal positions on time, memory, nature, will, culture, knowledge, and essential being. They reward study, too, as a capsule history of Byron's experience of the romantic vision, which he at first in a manner of speaking blindly recites, then positively enjoys and celebrates, then willynilly sees drift into a detached area of memory.

Many of Byron's lyrical positions turn out to bear comparison with those of Wordsworth, who it may be recalled was not unsympathetic to *Hours of Idleness.* "On a Distant View of the Village and School of Harrow on the Hill," though most readily associated with Gray's "Ode on a Distant Prospect of Eton College," is more meaningfully seen in relation to "Tintern Abbey"— the poem Wordsworth felt Bryon had laboriously used and "spoiled" in *Childe Harold*—or Coleridge's "Sonnet to the River Otter." Gray's "Ode" offers an ironic view of the "paradise" of "careless childhood," a flat and generally pessimistic opposition between "the little victims" and "men." As Patricia Meyer Spacks says, in this poem "we are offered the opposition, most dreadful of all, between youth and age, between the ignorance which provides hope and the wisdom which reveals futility, an opposition for which, in the nature of things, no reconciliation can be possible."[17] This is an attitude not unknown to Byron. But he is not guilty of it in "On a Distant View," which like "Tintern Abbey" loves and *trusts*

---

of the "Ode to a Lady whose Lover was Killed by a Ball" (*The Style of Don Juan*, New Haven, 1960, pp. 51ff.).

[17] " 'Artful Strife': Conflict in Gray's Poetry," *PMLA*, LXXXI (1966), 69.

the recollections of the past; they are "dreams . . . of boyhood" because he cannot now *realize* them—the temporal gap—and because he wishes he could, but *not* because he has misgivings as to their original reality. Again
like Wordsworth, Byron laments the loss in actuality of
boyhood's "pleasures," and asserts their immortality in
"ne'er fading remembrance." Though less systematically
than Wordsworth, Byron also finds in memory the possibility of partial recovery, partial redemption of present
loss: "Since darkness o'ershadows the prospect before
me, / More dear is the beam of the past to my soul." The
past for Byron is, perhaps typically, more social than for
Wordsworth, as he includes not only the natural scene of
hills and stream and field, but also the school and the
churchyard and even particular theatrical shows (sts.
5-6) which lead to an unWordsworthian humor: "I regard myself as a Garrick revived." Also, unlike the older
poet, Byron hints at the opening up of "new scenes of
pleasure" which may match the "scenes . . . of childhood."
The poem is effectively tenacious of childhood joys,
failing to balance its affirmative philosophy of childhood
with anything like Wordsworth's affirmative philosophy
of maturity.[18]

Still, "On a Distant View" looks forward with Words-
worth-Coleridge rather than backward to Gray. This, it
need hardly be said, is a judgment of its content and
mood; as poetry the piece can be summarized in words
applied to Addison's verse by Johnson: "it has not often
those felicities of diction which give lustre to sentiments,
or that vigor of sentiment that animates diction." The
crucial point, however, is that the eighteen-year-old

---

[18] This failing, found also in Coleridge's "Sonnet to the River
Otter," in no way adulterates the romanticism of the poem.

Byron, with no great finesse or feeling as a poet, correctly and sensitively carries out a romantic exercise, and concocts a Wordsworthian flavor. This gives a peculiar extension to a verdict he later passed on himself: "My earlier poems are the thoughts of one at least ten years older than the age at which they were written: I don't mean for their solidity, but their Experience" (*LJ*, v, 450). A natural aptitude, a receptivity on Byron's part to certain central terms of romanticism first manifests itself here.

Byron's assimilation of romantic tendencies of thought comes out in a most unexpected place, namely, in his relation to Pope. That relation has been gradually turning into a problematical one, with Eliot substituting Dunbar, John Wain substituting Burns, and Paul West substituting Diogenes for Pope as a positive influence on Byron, and with Ridenour curiously asserting Byron's "pious" devotion to the Augustans while demonstrating his "startling" divergence from the ways of Pope and Horace in the supposed act of following them (*The Style of Don Juan*, pp. 7, 36-38). Byron, as in his repeated demands for a poetry of truth, a poetry that was profitable to society, logical, and moral, seems typically to have made over the terms he undeniably borrowed from the Enlightenment. Truth for him carries little of the idea of tradition and authority, of standard and systematic values which are available and beneficial to the individual; it means candor and resolution in facing the voluminous problems of knowledge and experience. This is a cardinal and pervasive distinction. As regards the moral burden of literature, for example, when advised to suppress the early cantos of *Don Juan* on grounds of taste and morality, Byron bridled that it was "the first time" he had heard the word morality "from any body who was not a rascal that used it for a purpose" (*LJ*, IV, 479). One recognizes an opportunity to transfix him with an *argumentum ad hominem*, but it may be better to take another tack. Morality for Byron is not found in orthodox, behavioristic ways; in that sense, Donna Inez ranks high among the "moral," and it becomes necessary even to grant the horrendous "morality" of Glory and War. Byron's sense of morality is peculiarly epistemological, and rests on his conviction of the inscrutability of the universe, so that instead of formal obedience and a goal-directed self-discipline he appears to espouse self-honesty, personal generosity and if necessary self-sacrifice, spontaneity and inclusiveness of experience, and equilibrium in the face of human imperfection and incertitude. A harder and stricter style appears in his early works, such as *English Bards*, but in my judgment we see here his impulsive and even impure dislikes, not his considered moral view. We do not sufficiently stress the fact that he outgrew *English Bards*, a fairly shallow tyro's effort (*LJ*, III, 227 passim). To be sure he confessed to following a "wrong revolutionary poetical system" (*LJ*, v, 169). But if he called Gifford, whom he somewhat uncritically conceived of as an authentic upholder of Popean traditions, his "literary father," he also termed himself his "prodigal son" (*LJ*, VI, 329, 333), with no prospect of a homecoming.

How clearly then did Byron apprehend the difference between the wrong and the right poetical systems? We know that, far from insisting on the dichotomy of romanticism and classicism, he made a somewhat awkward, and "inconsistent" effort to scoff it out of existence:

'Classical' and 'Romantic' . . . were not subjects
of classification in England . . . when I left it
four or five years ago. Some of the English
Scribblers, it is true, abused Pope and Swift, . . .
but nobody thought them worth making a sect
of. Perhaps there may be something of the kind
sprung up lately, but . . . it would be such bad
taste that I should be very sorry to believe it.
> (*LJ*, v, 104)

More important yet, Byron found nothing intrinsically
wrong with contemporary poetry, and did not denounce
it outright. He was principally afraid of its effects on un-
wary successors, anticipating that "the next generation
(from the quantity and facility of imagination) will tum-
ble and break their necks off our Pegasus, who runs
away with us; but we keep the *saddle*, because we broke
the rascal and can ride. But though easy to mount, he
is the devil to guide" (*LJ*, IV, 197).

This relatively mild attitude gives way to an animated
depreciation of contemporary verse in the course of the
defenses of Pope. But is Byron's basic position therefore
altered? He did, after all, act as defender and not as
crusader—in fact he seems to have been drawn into the
controversy by Bowles's gratuitous invocation of his
name; and one may observe that he is less inclined to
reconcile his contemporaries to Pope than to reconcile
Pope's poetry with contemporary preferences.

For Byron's favorites among Pope's poems (e.g.,
Eloisa to Abelard) were typical of his day, and he liked
the qualities typically liked: softness, purity, passion,
beauty, and holiness (*LJ*, v, 581-582). He may have appreciated Pope as a poet of reason, but he urged his

countrymen not to let this quality get in the way of their appreciation of Pope's imagination and passion. Rarely is he concerned, in discussing the Augustan poet, with the Augustan standards of judgment, sense, propriety, moral, and design in poetry. He is concerned with emotion, and with emotion that borders on the indiscriminate. He speaks glowingly of the "imagery" of the *Epistle to Dr. Arbuthnot*, but shows withal little sense of Pope's aim. "The subject," he asserts, "is of no consequence (whether it be Satire or Epic)"—as if he conceived of Pope as merely seeking to put down lines "from which," as he himself puts it, "a painting might . . . be made" (*LJ*, v, 259-260). Even in *English Bards*, that ostensibly neo-Augustan poem, Pope is the writer whose "pure strain / Sought the rapt soul to charm, nor sought in vain." Byron holds up before detractors as a poet of "imagination" the man who had defined himself as having "stoop'd to Truth," and who had written to Swift on 19 December 1734:

> My system is a short one, and my circle narrow.
> Imagination has no limits, and that is a sphere
> in which you may move on to eternity; but where
> one is confined to truth, or, to speak more like a
> human creature, to the appearance of truth, we
> soon find the shortness of our tether.

Byron's romanticizing of Pope was hardly unique; it was the way of his age to praise Pope's command of "pathos" and "the moral sublime," to redefine in order to reclaim the neoclassical author. It is crucial to remember the vagaries of the Regency reception of the Augustan age, as shown by Mark Van Doren in his study of *John Dryden* and more extensively by Upali Amarasinghe in his *Dryden and Pope in the Early Nineteenth Century*. As things went, Augustan genius could be accommodated while Augustan correctness was cut away. If Pope defied rehabilitation, there was always Dryden to satisfy the craving for "orthodox" license.

In the final analysis Byron espouses a "classicism" so genial and so adventurous as to arrive at a near kinship with less extreme forms of romanticism, a classicism full of passion, sublimity, imagination, and individual genius. It is uncodified, uncrystallized, largely nominal classicism and no more makes Byron Popean (or, for that matter, Drydenesque), than his experiments with classical drama make him Greek. The fact that he championed Pope must, as far as major romantic poets go, remain singular, though we may recall Coleridge hesitating to condemn Pope comprehensively and Keats going to school to Dryden for the composition of *Lamia*. The reason that he championed him has something to do with sentimental associationism (he got his Pope young, and had a lifelong tendency to be fond of things of his youth); and something to do with romantic experimentalism, with his social suspicions of Wordsworth, and, as I have tried to show, with his declassicizing, unwittingly subversive conception of Pope.

How materially Byron developed a natural romantic aptitude can be seen in such poems as "To Edward Noel Long, Esq.," "Epistle to Augusta," and "I Would I Were a Careless Child." The first of these, by a certain arch self-consciousness in the fourth and in parts of the fifth stanza, perhaps betrays itself to be another product of Byron's "infant Muse." But this disability is more than offset as the poem demonstrates a deeper and more sensitive use of nature, and of poetic language and structure, than "On a Distant View," as well as a more elaborate knowledge of the links between past and present joys.

> Dear Long, in this sequester'd scene
> While all around in slumber lie,
> The joyous days which ours have been
> Come rolling fresh on Fancy's eye. . . .
>
> . . . .
>
> Though Youth has flown on rosy pinion,
> And Manhood claims his stern dominion—
> Age will not every hope destroy,
> But yield some hours of sober joy.

The spirit as well as the ring of these lines, bating the problematical "Fancy," will almost inevitably conjure up thoughts of Wordsworth. We sense the world of "Tintern Abbey" where the "wild ecstasies" of youth mature "into a sober pleasure." Byron has "sequestration" to Wordsworth's "seclusion." He writes, "all around in slumber lie"; Wordsworth, in his more intricately woven work, accumulates the evidence of slumber all around with his "soft inland murmur," "quiet of the sky," "repose," and "silence." Both poets make seclusion and repose not only a setting for actors but also a vital condition for reflection and insight. Both also qualify their solitude by use of an alter ego,[19] contriving thereby to give

---

[19] Long is used fairly straightforwardly by Byron as a companion in the past and a sure present corroborator of its truth:

> Yes, as you knew me in the days
> O'er which Rememberance yet delays,
> Still may I rove, untutored, wild.
> And even in age at heart a child.

Byron here suggests not only the Wordsworthian paradox of wishing to combine memory with an untutored, unaffected state, and be

nature a "human center," a human fulfillment. At the end of his poem Byron again turns farther than Wordsworth in a social direction; his version of a removal from youthful purity seems to be the picture of "daliaunce and fayre langage" in the fourth stanza. But he does not lose his sense of identification with Long or of *their* involvement with memory and nature. The rest of the faceless festive crew in which they "mingle" presumably do not have the same *spiritual* experience as they.[20] The moon, for them, is no casual factor. It is a redeeming agent whose light chases away "the gloom profound" that is at once literal and metaphysical—darkness in the first stanza is definitely associated with the present, and with day, as "clouds the darken'd noon deform"; and this association appears again at the close of the poem when the propitious moon fades and one is caught in "the mist [the unreliable light] of morn." Byron's "sacred intellectual shower," social in context as it is, remains a personal, mystical phenomenon under the aegis of the moon which in nature transcends and for us rescinds awhile time's natural consequences:

"even in age at heart a child," but also the poignant blending of energy and radical self-doubt in such a wish. "Still may I rove" is simultaneously a statement of permission or liberty and a confession of disability, a wish.

[20] An arresting picture of Byron's aloof participation in festivity and also of his burdened sense of the privations of age is provided in his "Detached Thoughts":

I mingled with, and dined and supped, etc., with them [companions at Cambridge]; but, I know not how, it was one of the deadliest and heaviest feelings of my life to feel that I was no longer a boy. From that moment I began to grow old in my own esteem; and in my esteem age is not estimable (*LJ*, v, 445).

. . . Ere yon silver lamp of night
Has thrice perform'd her stated round,
Has thrice retraced her path of light,
And chased away the gloom profound,
I trust that we, my gentle friend,
Shall see her rolling orbit wend
Above the dear-loved peaceful seat
Which once contained our youth's retreat;

.　.　.　.　.　.　.　.　.　.　.　.

And all the flow of souls shall pour
The sacred intellectual shower,
Nor cease till Luna's waning horn
Scarce glimmers through the mist of morn.

The influence not only of the mist of morn but of the darkened and cloud-deformed noon was not always to be denied in Byron's experience. Memory and nature, without losing their powers, lose their efficacy; we find them curiously inert in the "Epistle to Augusta," which is significantly the latest of the poems under discussion. Here the redemption of time appears incalculably remote. Byron, less wise and less passive than Wordsworth, has brought on his own alienation: "I have been cunning in my overthrow, / The careful pilot of my proper woe." His knowledge that his woe is deserved (one meaning of "proper") in no way leads toward redemption. Even his knowledge of the way of redemption through nature and memory (sts. 7-8) proves futile. But that knowledge possesses all the poignancy and stature of Coleridge's "I see, not feel, how beautiful they are!" The poem, as Oliver Elton states, "is grave and beautiful in finish";[21]

[21] "Byron," in *A Survey of English Literature*: 1780-1880, Vol. II, New York, 1920, 159.

that finish serves to bring home and clinch, esthetically, the dark emotional and moral burden of the "Epistle." Byron goes beyond Coleridge and Wordsworth in recognizing the will, the individual's conscious deeds, as thwarting the potential reconciliation between man and nature, man and his existence in altering time. This recognition constitutes a special contribution to the philosophy of the romantic lyric, or indeed to romantic philosophy.

The lyric "I Would I Were a Careless Child" also centers around the possibility of fusing knowledge, memory, and nature into a philosophical recovery of the losses of time. That possibility is not negated here, but neither is it fully realized. The poem occupies the middle ground between "To Edward Noel Long, Esq." and the "Epistle to Augusta." It shows not will, but sheer circumstances upsetting man's innocence. It presents not a scene of recovery, but a state of desire. The subjunctive mood with which it begins ("I would I were . . .") effectively controls its amplitude. A "festive crew" appears in a light very different from that in "To Edward Noel Long, Esq."

> Though gay companions o'er the bowl
> Dispel awhile the sense of ill;
> Though pleasure stirs the maddening soul,
> The heart—the heart—is lonely still.

The poem, it may be useful to note, commences from the point at which Coleridge's "Sonnet to the River Otter" ends:

> I would I were a careless child,
> Still dwelling in my Highland cave,

Or roving through the dusky wild,
Or bounding o'er the dark blue wave;[22]
The cumbrous pomp of Saxon pride
Accords not with the freeborn soul,
Which loves the mountain's craggy side,
And seeks the rocks where billows roll.

But the gifts of nature, original innocence and spontaneous belonging in nature, have been supplanted by
the gifts of fortune. What is gained seems worthless
beside what is lost, and the poem poignantly cries to
fortune to revoke its own gifts and restore those of nature. The eight-line stanza is divided equally between
the two wishes, with an almost perfect antithesis between the halves: present vs. past, "cultured lands" vs.
"the rocks," hate vs. love, slaves ceaselessly cringing
around vs. freedom to rove, a "name of splendid sound"
vs. the sound of the wild Ocean.

Fortune! take back these cultured lands,
Take back this name of splendid sound!
I hate the touch of servile hands,
I hate the slaves that cringe around.
Place me among the rocks I love,
Which sound to Ocean's wildest roar;
I ask but this—again to rove
Through scenes my youth hath known before.

Clearly the stanza is dealing with loss of liberty on various levels, for more is at stake than "the license to roam

---

[22] The obscurity common to the three settings, "cave" and
"dusky wild" and "dark blue wave," bears noticing; it must be
distinguished from the "gloom" that "may suit" the speaker's
now "darken'd mind." There is nothing pat or mechanical about
Byron's use of the image of darkness here, or elsewhere in his
poetry.

at will."[23] The boy who was free to rove with *the* free ("wild") Ocean as setting and standard finds himself a man limited to his lands and implicitly hemmed in by the very servants who, in the "cultured" context, should release him from care. Worse than this, in his attendants (or flatterers, perhaps) he beholds undisguised the last implications of being without liberty. They are not servants but "servile," "slaves that cringe." To hate their degraded condition—he does not hate them in themselves —is to keep in some degree free from culture, or corruption. But, unfortunately, not to be free.

The menace of the cultured context, it develops, can have positive benefits. For just as Wordsworth at Cambridge, under a challenge to his natural possession of liberty and unity in nature, is obliged to comprehend and affirm that possession, the speaker in "I Would I Were a Careless Child" must face his assumptions and define his position. He learns, like Wordsworth, that he "was not for that hour, / Nor for that place" (*The Prelude* IV. 81-82). Simultaneously he learns the essential quality of the hour and place he *was* for, but which he will not know again. Byron's lines seem remarkably close to the "Ode: Intimations of Immortality":[24]

> Few are my years, and yet I feel
> The world was ne'er design'd for me:
> Ah! why do dark'ning shades conceal
> The hour when man must cease to be?

[23] Bernard Blackstone, *The Lost Travellers: A Romantic Theme with Variations*, London, 1962, p. 189.

[24] For a review of the prompt and profound influence of this poem on the poetry and thinking of the first half of the nineteenth century, the reader is referred to Barbara Garlitz' "The Immortality Ode: Its Cultural Progeny," *SEL*, VI (1966), 639-649.

Once I beheld a splendid dream,
A visionary scene of bliss:
Truth!—wherefore did thy hated beam
Awake me to a world like this?

Here truth, like fortune above, is the ironic and anti-pathetic concept. Its beam is no better than "dark'ning shades," the world it reveals is "design'd" not created, formal not free: "Reality's dark dream."

Two factors prevent a resolution of the speaker's dilemma: the absence of a Long or Dorothy to engage him and turn him from his present desolation toward the continuing viability of the past, and the inability of the solitary will to serve the turn. For though man must diligently lay hold of what he has in nature, he must also keep time with the rhythm with which nature freely gives; there is no ordering a custom model of experience, pat to the singular heart's desire. "Dejection: An Ode" bears witness to the inefficacy of mere will. So do Wordsworth's empirical faith in "wise passiveness" and his definition of beatitude of being as a state with no *particular* will. It is typical of romanticism that the function of the will proves injurious in the "Ode: Intimations of Immortality" (st. vi), and is beneficial accidentally, not intrinsically, in such as the rowboat scene and the Mt. Snowdon episode in *The Prelude*: the unanticipated educative gift of nature counters or cuts across Wordsworth's purposes in each case. A precocious sense of the imperviousness of circumstances to the play of the will emerges from "I Would I Were a Careless Child." The speaker, confined to "cultured lands," and doubly portcullised from the liberty of nature by "servile hands" and "slaves that cringe around," predictably ends on a note of sorrowing velleity:

Fain would I fly the haunts of men—
I seek to shun, not hate mankind;
My breast requires the sullen glen,
Whose gloom may suit a darken'd mind.
Oh! that to me the wings were given
Which bear the turtle to her nest!
Then would I cleave the vault of heaven,
To flee away, and be at rest.

The poems just considered begin, I think, to give color to the conception of Byron as a romantic lyrist, showing him at once more spontaneously and more richly concerned with the problems of time, memory, knowledge, and nature than he is usually given credit for. He did not, of course, recover his place and poise in nature. Of those who agonized over the loss, only Wordsworth recovered, and he only with laborious patience and self-dedication. By and large the desire for "the sullen glen, / Whose gloom may suit a darken'd mind" gets its literary fulfillment in Byron. The attitude we see in his desire to "shun, not hate mankind" curdles into *Manfred* with its disdainful view of man and exalted view of the very will which in the "Epistle to Augusta" denaturalizes man. When Manfred speaks of "My Mother Earth," it is fair to say that he is indulging in a name of splendid sound. Byron's passing ejaculations of reunion with nature, as for example in *Childe Harold* III, quite fail to bridge the practical abyss between faith in nature as a vital power and mere acknowledgment of nature as a potentially vital power. And Byron was fully aware of this. He is ready to profess himself "a lover of Nature and an admirer of Beauty," but no less prompt in admitting that "neither the music of the Shepherd, the crashing of the

Avalanche, nor the torrent, the mountain, the Glacier, the Forest, nor the Cloud, have for one moment lightened the weight upon my heart, nor enabled me to lose my own wretched identity in the majesty, and the power, and the Glory, around, above, and beneath me" (*LJ*, III, 364). Fortune, and that skepticism which took hold in his mind and inhibited his ability to derive conviction from commitment, usually shut nature off for Byron as a serene and generous home.[25]

But of course that exclusion, or loss, is entirely in keeping with the pattern of romantic experience of nature. For the latter does not merely replace the old classical (and largely limited and horizontal) formality of response to nature with a mystical (and frequently limitless, vertical) concentration; it also shows, instead of the axiological clarity and assurance of the classical response, a new sense of the precariousness of nature's powers, or at least of man's fruitful perception thereof. Finders of something new in nature, the romantics were less than successful keepers.

A substantial conception of nature and of the mind, and of their mutual relation in the modifying circumstances of time and place has been seen as the radical content of a number of Byron's lyrics. In *Hebrew Melodies* one finds that conception tacitly assumed and applied, and also significantly complemented with a philosophy of art. "The Harp the Monarch Minstrel Swept" may be taken as exemplary. The poem, which may appear merely atavistic as a type of *encomium musicae*, is remarkable as a cogent revival and transformation of

[25] A full-scale treatment of Byron's deteriorated responses to nature is provided by Ernest J. Lovell, Jr., in *Byron: The Record of a Quest*, Austin, Texas, 1949.

that venerable fashion. The ordinary distinction between king and musician, to which Dryden lends his authority, is canceled in the oxymoron of "monarch minstrel"; here excellence in music is to surpass and cap excellence in arms: "David's Lyre grew mightier than his Throne." Similarly the power of music proves to be less than a virtuoso one, able to make men match its own gamut of emotions.[26] It does produce contradictions, but within a definite humane or ethical system of values: "It soften'd men of iron mould, / It gave them virtues not their own." In a cryptic paradox combining secular power and divine favor, David is at once "The King of men" and "the loved of Heaven"; and his music, the poem's music, is "hallow'd" rather than aesthetic or cosmic. So wholly does David act within a universal moral context that, when his music tells of "the triumphs of our King," he is as much the King as Christ, under whom he is king. In a quiet and decisive way, Bryon is reversing the historical pattern which had led to the "minimization of the cosmological significance of the music of the spheres."[27]

Still, it is clear that Byron's view of music is less religious than prototypal. The focus of the poem becomes the sacred and unique moment hypostatized in music, and its relation to a time obscurely reflecting back on that moment. David's music embodies immortality in music. That immortality, lost in fact, is preserved somehow in memory, which thereby serves as a defense against the experience of mortality. "The Harp" is thus revealed as a special parallel to the poem "To Edward

[26] Instead of making men feel everything, music makes all men feel: "No ear so dull, no soul so cold, / That felt not, fired not to the tone, / Till David's Lyre grew mightier than his Throne."
[27] John Hollander, *The Untuning of the Sky: Ideas of Music in English Poetry, 1500-1700*, Princeton, New Jersey, 1961, p. 358.

Noel Long, Esq." The parallel gets significantly extended as "The Harp" contrives, by a sort of semi-synaesthesia, to transfer the idealized musical context into the visual terms of light and dark, the more typical vehicle for its near-mystical statement:

Since then,[28] though heard on earth no more,
Devotion and her daughter Love
Still bid the bursting spirit soar
To sounds that seem as from above,
In dreams that day's broad light can not remove.

The failure of daylight to remove the dreams[29] amounts to the failure of mortality to get the better of immortality. The music, after all, only *seems* "as from above." It is partly with us yet. For "dreams" must carry the definition enunciated by Coleridge, the "semblance of some unknown past, like to a dream, and not 'a semblance *presented* in a dream'" (*Letters*, I, 167). The bursting spirit soars *up towards*, but also in *direct response to* the music, for if it is ideal it is also somehow familiar: something we have known. Indeed, it appears that we

[28] The sound of the harp, the poem has said, "aspired to Heaven and there abode."

[29] Another of the *Hebrew Melodies*, "She Walks in Beauty," also disparages daylight ("gaudy day") and favors instead the night of "cloudless climes and starry skies." Such a night, like the "aspect" and "eyes" of the poem's subject, embraces "All that's best of dark and bright." The fusion of the opposites of dark and bright is matter-of-factly stated, but it is a mysterious thing. Only the "best of dark and bright" comes into play, so that neither term really has its natural meaning: they are idealized terms. Something timeless, preternatural hangs about the night and the lady alike. The "beauty" *in* which she is said to walk is also essential and timeless. That "beauty," "the night" and "she" interpenetrate and become interchangeable in an uncanny identification of a human being with a phenomenal state and an abstraction. The ostensibly simple rhetoric asserts nature, achieves mysticism.

· 28 ·

first created it, even if it was to make "Heaven" its "abode." Byron spends a relatively large proportion of the poem's twenty verses on Orphic music and heavenly music, but without making these his chief concern. They are forms of the first human excellence, which was not infused, but implicit. Its "chords are riven," of course; yet memory and language effectively revive and consecrate it, unto eternity, in the very teeth of the materialistic assumption of a strict, finite succession of things, of a past that is gone and done with. The truth of memory puts down the nihilistic suppositions of logic; the truth of "dreams" withstands "day's broad light," as the poem posits an extra-scientific theory that experience is not destroyed but translated into invisible but still available terms. Mythic in impulse, it humanizes and romanticizes its classical and Christian myths. Its "dreams" are of a perfectly human past, and latently also, I think, of a like future.[30] Like poetry, music offers "the feeling of a Former world and a Future" (LJ, v, 189).

[30] Even allowing for Byron's usual fluency in composition, his prompt and flawless execution of these last five lines of the poem, which bring us "down again" from Heaven (Isaac Nathan, *Fugitive Pieces*, London, 1828, p. 30), may well betoken the ripeness of the humanistic idea in his mind. Nor is such a human orientation out of place; it is by inertia that Byron's lyrics retain the general title of Hebrew Melodies, with which their association was never very close or profound. As E. H. Coleridge points out, less than half of the pieces were composed in accordance with Byron's agreement to provide lyrics for music scored by Isaac Nathan and to be sung by John Braham (PW, iii, 375). The reviewers of the *Analectic Magazine*, vi (1815), 292-294 and of the *Christian Observer*, xiv (1815), 542-549 found the poems at best vaguely scriptural. But then neither poet nor musician labored under an illusion about the matter. When Nathan asked Byron how "Oh! Snatch'd Away in Beauty's Bloom" might "refer to any scriptural subject," Byron "appeared for a moment affected," then fudged an answer: "Every mind must make its own reference" (Nathan, p. 30).

The little span from dreams to daylight repeats in miniature the considerable span of time between "then" and "since." History is imaged in less than a natural day, and in turn both general history and singular day image and are implicitly imaged in a third span: that of the single life going, as in "Tintern Abbey" or "To Edward Noel Long, Esq.," from integrated youth to alienated manhood. Like nature in those poems, art, ideally conceived, reveals to us and preserves for us knowledge of our place outside of mutable time, whose light is obscurity. More than this, art withstands time for us; we withstand time through it, and are restored, albeit partially and temporarily, to our extratemporal place.

Such a view of art underlies yet another of the *Hebrew Melodies*, "My Soul Is Dark," which also involves the semi-synaesthesia of a vision created by a sound. But critical details have changed. Instead of the abstract, almost communal voice of "The Harp," this poem offers a vividly self-conscious speaker who knows better things than he has.

> My soul is dark—Oh! quickly string
> The harp I yet can brook to hear;
> And let thy gentle fingers fling
> Its melting murmurs o'er mine ear.
> If in this heart a hope be dear,
> That sound shall charm it forth again:
> If in these eyes there lurk a tear,
> 'T will flow, and cease to burn my brain.
> But bid the strain be wild and deep,
> Nor let thy notes of joy be first:
> I tell thee, minstrel, I must weep,
> Or else this heavy heart will burst;

For it hath been by sorrow nursed,
And ached in sleepless silence long;
And now 't is doom'd to know the worst,
And break at once—or yield to song.

It is left uncertain whether he is saved from darkness and suffering by the harp. He certainly expects, and urgently desires, to be. No doubt arises as to the power of the harp, and little doubt is encouraged as to the receptivity of the speaker. The crucial element in the poem would once again appear to be the will. The hearer knows his state, and its danger, both emotional and intellectual (burning brain, overladen heart). He knows he "must weep," must lose himself to save himself emotionally and intellectually for some imaginable future: "If in this heart a hope be dear. . . ." The implication is that something will necessarily follow "if" the stated condition is met. The precondition embodied in music is compounded (but bid the strain be wild . . .) and further compounded (nor let the notes of joy be first); and then, when it would seem that so precise a formulation must guarantee success, we come upon the possibility of its being altogether too late: his heart may be "doom'd" to "break." This sort of practical uncertainty is bound up with a pair of philosophical paradoxes in "My Soul Is Dark," with its dramatization of the will to surrender the will, of the self-conscious mind striving to yield away the self. Add to these the paradox of the dream which is truer than day, and a radical problem of knowledge and belief appears.

The title of the poem suggests a pre-mystical state, but it is an arrested pre-mysticism, at once too analytically conscious and too doubtful of the means to a saving self-transcendence. The present material reality—the power of pain—is locked at a point of crisis with the immanent, timeless reality of the power of music (and it may offer a presage of the future that this conflict of two realities or schemes of knowledge remains unresolved; Byron will again be caught between the claims of actuality and hope). Music and pain, both undeniable, cannot both survive, but the poem cannot settle the issue. Its palpable instrument is will, which we see as isolating and incapable of redeeming itself, though the definite fear that the present could negate the immanent places the poem on the side of the angels.

The want of a definite solution in "My Soul Is Dark" is perhaps supplied in "The Destruction of Sennacherib," where the pervasive similes suggest that nature, or a general will, favors innocence as an ordained state over the contingent state of terror. Naïve and mechanically "Biblical" though they may seem in terms of today's literary predilections, these similes subtly define the universe of the poem. First they suggest a certain ordinariness or typicality in nature: "The Assyrian came down like the wolf on the fold," "And the gleam of their [his cohorts'] spears was like stars on the sea, / When the blue wave rolls nightly. . . ." A sort of delayed tension, developing with the apprehension that it is war which gets defined as ordinary or "natural," is both reflected and reinforced in the conflict of the natural trope: the wolf vs. the fold. Tension in nature recurs in the second stanza, between "leaves of the forest when Summer is green" and "leaves of the forest when Autumn hath blown." But a crucial reorientation takes place here. The activity and purpose involved in the wolf-fold metaphor give way to the passivity of the cycling leaves, a passivity emphasized in the static and passive phrasing: "are seen" and "lay wither'd and strown." Moreover, the metaphor of the leaves refers *in both instances* to the Assyrian host, who in the first stanza so fiercely "came down" on the lamb-like enemy. Still in a pattern of nature, they find their activity and will superseded by a higher and less momentary principle. The more or less horizontal tension, wolf vs. fold, is revised into a vertical one, leaves (raised banners) vs. leaves (fallen host), or rather into an abstract tension between the partial present and an eternal perfection, between self-will and the implicit will of Nature; a certain quality of ignorance and presumption in the Assyrians is revealed when they are called "sleepers." The subjection of the aggressor to Nature appears graphically as the erstwhile rider "lay . . . distorted and pale,[31] / With the *dew* on his brow and the *rust* on his mail" (italics added). The negation of his activity reveals itself in "the lances *unlifted*, the trumpet *unblown*" (italics added); the participles, as a contemporary reviewer felt, make "lagging lazy words."[32] It is noticeable, too, that his enemy, though successful, is no more active, as the Gentile falls "unsmote by the sword." Nature itself in the form of the "blast," as something exceeding and superseding human agency, is what fells the Gentiles. Actually the natural manifests the supernatural. But to the last the poem's rhetoric orients us toward the natural world:

And the might of the Gentile, unsmote by the sword,
Hath *melted like snow* in the glance of the Lord.

[31] No longer does he gleam "in purple and gold."
[32] "Hebrew Melodies, by Lord Byron," *Christian Observer*, xiv (1815), 547.

Rhetorically it is in terms of, and through, a complex but consistent nature that the supernatural occurrence unfolds and has meaning. The similes are not ornamental but instrumental, serving to inform the simple if strange story with a philosophy that is complex, yet clear.[33]

In the light of the readings set forth here, a significant number of Byron's lyrics would take a place in the romantic category. They do so not only in terms of philosophy, but also in terms of rhetoric, with an ostensibly naive surface of form and language manifesting an essentially knowledgeable and complex position. Perhaps Byron's lyrics have "suffered" more than those of his major contemporaries from what Earl R. Wasserman sees as a typical crux of the romantic lyric, "the superficial appearance of not requiring an intensive metaphysical reading"; for it proves true often enough with the uncelebrated Byron, as with the rest, that "it is . . . not merely in the overt statements, often disarmingly simple, but especially in the inner subtleties of [the] language . . . that we must seek the articulation of" a poem's fullest meaning.[34]

It would bear stressing, however, that such lyrics stand in no pat relation to the great body of Byron's work. He articulates no propaedeutic *Prelude*. He does not, like Wordsworth, have an "Old Cumberland Beggar" to clarify a cryptic line ("Stop here, or gently pass") in "The Solitary Reaper." His poetic manifesto, if the "Reply to *Blackwood's*" can be so called, tends to obfuscate

---

[33] The reader should compare G. Wilson Knight's suggestive, if fulsome reading of this poem in his *Byron and Shakespeare*, New York, 1966, pp. 13-15, and Robert F. Gleckner's reading, in *Byron and the Ruins of Paradise*, with its isolating focus on a "landscape of death" and "victory hollow and wintry," Baltimore, Maryland, 1967, p. 209.

[34] *The Subtler Language*, Baltimore, Maryland, 1959, p. 252.

the issues it pretends to define: his own poetic principles, Pope's poetry, and contemporary poetic philosophy and prejudice. In a special way Byron's romantic lyrics stand alone.

We see the positive view of nature in "The Destruction of Sennacherib" countervailed in *Childe Harold* (III. xxvii-xxx), the view of war there diminished from a faith to an indignant hope in the cantos on the Siege of Ismail in *Don Juan*. The idealism as to youth and nature that we see in "To Edward Noel Long, Esq." succumbs to the sense of *process*, of irreversible time, in *Manfred* and *Don Juan* alike. The will loses all fruitful relation to the universe, which appears irrational, in "Prometheus." Defiance, a negative value of will, becomes a keynote of *Manfred* and a significant element in *Childe Harold* (III.xii).

The universal view of art found in "The Harp" and "My Soul Is Dark" suffers a sardonic revision in *Don Juan*:

> . . . *wild* as an Aeolian harp,
> With which the winds of heaven *can* claim accord,
> And make *a* music, *whether flat or sharp*.
> (XIII.xciii: italics added)

Even before this, art's universality had been turned inward and downward to subjectivity in *Childe Harold* III (st. iv) and again, in *Don Juan*:

> And the unquiet feelings, which first woke
> Song in the world, will seek what then they sought;
> As on the beach the waves at last are broke,
> Thus to the extreme verge the passions brought
> Dash into poetry, which is but passion. . . .
> (IV.cvi)

Art, arising from passion and exploiting the will, can even become divorced from the actualities of existence and fashion its own system. Byron writes in "The Prophesy of Dante":

> . . . What is Poesy but to create
> From overfeeling Good and Ill; and aim
> At an external life beyond our fate,
> And be the new Prometheus of new men. . . ?

The "overfeeling," or ecstasy, gives definition to both the "aim" and the "external life": they are *beyond* and *separate from* the here and now. The poem offers no real hope for the new Prometheus or the new men.[35] Poesy, this version of creation, bids fair to yield a solipsistic system, not a universe.

The affirmations of the romantic lyrics, however, hold an integral place beside the inversions and oppositions met elsewhere in the Byron corpus. Byron's notorious "mobility," we might say, has its intellectual aspect, enabling and perhaps impelling him to recognize the mul-

---

[35] This phrase hardly seems suitable to Dante or congruous with the Christian overview informing the poem's opening lines and recurring throughout the first cantos. Byron's "new man" has his place far from the *novus homo* of Christian thought, just as Prometheus belongs in a dissonant mythology. While invoking another philosophy, the final canto does not redefine or transcend that which has been at work before. This change-without-continuity entails a certain incoherence and weakens the poem's impact. Without denying the speaker's "sense of ultimate personal fulfillment" (Marshall, *The Structure*, p. 135), one may well challenge the validity of that sense; the prophecy would seem to be demanded by the emotional needs of the speaker, and not finally justified either by his intellectual and spiritual character or by the philosophical terms diffused through the poem. The poem, of course, as prophecy legitimately seeks an incantatory possession rather than a systematic persuasion of the reader; but it strikes me as appropriate to scrutinize and judge the recourses of prophecy, especially that of another day.

tiplicity of tenable positions. Among these, paradoxically, belongs the faith in unity expressed principally in a handful of lyrics in the romantic mode. Through them we can recognize that Byron's "general antagonism . . . to anything hinting of the mystical or the incomprehensible"[36] is not obsessive or uninformed, but perhaps bespeaks an acceptance of the rarity and brevity of the genuine thing, and a suspicion of what he himself might have termed Joanna Southcote "mystery and mysticism" in deceived or deceitful persons (*LJ*, III, 239).

[36] Ernest J. Lovell, Jr., *Byron*, p. 67.

THE FRAGMENTED SHAPES
OF ORDER:
CHILDE HAROLD III

You can't go home again. THOMAS WOLFE

No one but Byron has ever thought of the third canto of *Childe Harold* as a mere continuation of a poem he had "but begun" (III.iii).[1] On the contrary there are some who would put a mischievous construction on the protestation: "it may be that in vain / I would essay as I have sung to sing" (iv). For Byron's writing, his singing, had undergone a change since the morning when he awoke and found himself famous. It had become substantially richer in thought, feeling, and style. In his handling of the persons met in *Childe Harold* III, for example, we find none of the high-handed partiality of the beginner satires, none of the straitening, feverish brooding of the tales, and, most notably, none of the spectral abstraction of the first two cantos. In the opening cantos places take precedence over people; the mature Byron would declare that places and things acquire interest from human associations alone. The Spanish maid (I.liv ff.) stands out in three dimensions among amorphous Tyrants, despots, Monarchs, chieftains, and battle's minions. She lives and moves and is a being where the hero, the Mighty, the muleteer, the warrior, the sophist, the saint, sage, and prophet (I-II, passim)

---

[1] On this subject it should suffice to recall Gifford's sentiment that what Byron had published before was "nothing to this effort" (*PW*, II, 212).

freeze in instant abstraction and generalization.[2] In the new canto Byron is at home individualizing and analyzing a variety of historical characters and situations. Even then his greatest advance is more than numerical. He shows a remarkable deftness and tact in arranging the subjects of his analysis, playing them off against one another, so that their relation becomes tacitly dialogistic in a rudimentary politico-philosophical drama.

As striking as this kind of development may seem, it has been almost inevitably eclipsed by changes on a higher, thematic level in *Childe Harold* III, and in particular by a change in Byron's attitude toward Nature. There is a certain suddenness about his formal avowal of faith in the transcendental operations of Nature; one's attention is seized by the novelty of it, and no less strongly seized by the conspicuous new link with two major contemporaries, Shelley and Wordsworth. But that avowal has not sustained either itself or the critical imagination. Instead it has come to be thought of as impetuous and artificial. It may be fairly convincing as an index of yearning or need for transcendence through Nature; it is far less convincing as proof, or even as a promise of such transcendence.

The idea long current in criticism is that *Childe Harold* III constitutes an abortive quest on Byron's part for what was in his case a new transcendental position. So serenely is this idea held that writers on other romantic

---

[2] The enhancement on the artistic level comes with, and probably to some extent comes from Byron's breaking away from the mechanical sequence of time and space on the pilgrimage (see William A. Borst, *Lord Byron's First Pilgrimage*, New Haven, 1948, pp. 22-23). As Borst says, "*Childe Harold* becomes a better poem as the dependence upon fairly precise detail is subordinated to a more emotional shaping of the material" (p. 23).

poets invoke it *en passant* to make definitive comparisons with Byron; thus Herbert Lindenberger asserts that in *Childe Harold* III (st. lxxii) Byron "is *working toward* the expression of a type of experience completely foreign to his real talent."[3] This amounts to a truth freighted with false implications. For Byron in 1816 cannot legitimately pass as a would-be convert to transcendentalism; he has embodied that faith in important lyrics before 1816. The composer of "To Edward Noel Long, Esq.," "The Harp the Monarch Minstrel Swept," "My Soul Is Dark," and "The Destruction of Sennacherib" would appear rather as a prodigal son cocking his ear for breathings from home.

The new canto of *Childe Harold* directs itself toward *recovering*, not discovering, an extra-mundane view. More than this, the new canto betrays a continual consciousness that its transcendentalism is transcendentalism manqué, and that desire for a given relation to Nature falls subject to so many adversities as to be lost to the realm of will[4] and subside into simple velleity. This will prove true of all other relations explored in the canto, which is at last most remarkable for the number of sanctuaries it shows Byron vainly seeking: the usual critical focus on the sanctuary of Nature, however understandable in the context of romanticism, has been somewhat unfortunate in taking that sanctuary out of the context of the poem. One notes, too, that while elements of Nature appear often and prominently in the canto, they hardly cohere into a describable, substantial,

[3] *On Wordsworth's Prelude*, Princeton, New Jersey, 1963, p. 49; italics added.

[4] For a different and perhaps more common view of will in this poem, the reader should consult Pafford's "Byron and the Mind of Man."

unified conception. Perhaps it would be more than a semantic quibble to ask to what extent Nature, thus dismantled and disjointed, remains Nature at all. As Ward Pafford remarks, "interest in nature per se comes to be incidental to a questioning of its relation and value to the living mind" ("Mind of Man," 111). Beyond seeing that it concerns itself overtly with a possible transcendental view of Nature, or of elements thereof, one would judge that agnosticism is what *Childe Harold* III asserts.

This conclusion is obviously to be derived from the way Byron's most ambitiously sweeping statements concerning even the transitory attractions in Nature continually get hobbled by conditions and concessions. It receives powerful corroboration from the way a basic changeableness marks, or mars the narrative viewpoint, making it as important to see what the poem betrays as what is says, as crucial to comprehend what is revealed by the sequence of statements as the formal content of the statements by themselves. Analysis of the tangled structural surface of *Childe Harold* III becomes paramount for an understanding of Byron's total attitude. Because of its statistical prominence, the following pages deal heavily with the familiar topic of "Nature," but they seek to describe and evaluate a symptomatic tangle, in which semblances of order—the framing stanzas on Byron's daughter or, on another level, philosophical transcendentalism—prove otiose and are hardly even asked to dissimulate the central disarray of Byron's experience. In limited sections and in accumulated units, in characterization and in imagery *Childe Harold* III appears at odds with itself, embodying a temper that is at once calculating and hysterical, skeptical and compulsive, and systematic and random. It presents a study of a man reconnoitering avenues to emotional and moral security when he knows he contains in himself the insuperable barrier to success. That man is indifferently Byron or Childe Harold, who obviously "re-appears" because Byron is again a'wandering. He is not a "persona" but Byron's self-impersonation.[5]

The impasse presents itself at once in the stanzas leading up to, or rather preceding Byron's first great utterance of nature mysticism ("Where rose the mountains," etc.). These stanzas propose an alternative to Nature as a source of self-transcendence, and that alternative implicitly devalues Nature. In addition, the stanzas in question help to test the natural philosophy that is professed, by what they tell of the professor's mentality and motives. Above all, in the use they make of Nature in crucial metaphors, they suggest a despairing conception of man's relation to her and thus undermine the identification posited in stanza xiii. Again, it is not so much the expressed themes as the revealed method, the process of the speaking intellect, that should be taken as basic here.

The alternative to Nature is art. Not art itself, as no recourse will prove less tenuous or more definitive than Nature in the poem; we find that Byron's "art" means not the timeless product of cognitive and imaginative and emotional endeavor, but rather the complex temporal act

---

[5] While admitting that the "similarities" between Byron and Childe Harold in this third canto "are rife," and while hesitating to contend that Byron "consciously pioneered a modern [narrative] technique," Kenneth A. Bruffee attempts to schematize a functional and substantive difference between Byron and Childe Harold as a matter of Byron's doing ("The Synthetic Hero and the Narrative Structure of *Childe Harold* iii," *SEL*, vi [1966], 669-678). It seems likelier that the unstable relation of the two in the poem further illustrates a pervasive difficulty of orientation.

of composition or "creation" (sts. iv-vi). Byron's expectations, one is struck to find, differ little whether he looks to Nature or to art-as-activity; and he looks to the latter first in the canto, and also, in biographical terms, longest. Even apart from the fact that he turns to Nature "on the rebound" (st. xii), it is hard to see her as a substantive force for him when she offers relief no less periodical than composing verse, and no more intrinsic. And vice versa.

Salient features of the resort to Nature in *Childe Harold* III come together in the opening verses of stanza xiv:

> Like the Chaldean he [Harold] could watch the stars,
> Till he had peopled them with beings bright
> As their own beams; and earth, and earth-born jars,
> And human frailties, were forgotten quite.
> Could he have kept his spirit to that flight
> He had been happy....[6]

The goal, to forget; the means, withdrawal into an ecstasy of imaginary (not imaginative) brightness and ethereality; the prospect, disappointment à la Icarus. The resumption of the poem has entailed the same syndrome. The goal of forgetfulness is poignantly expressed in stanza iv:

---

[6] These lines separate themselves from the preceding stanza in fairly striking ways. In them Nature serves as a catalyst, perhaps even as a merely contingent setting, making terms like "friends," "home," "companionship," and "mutual language" seem generally incongruous. In them Childe Harold's state gets graphic realization. It is almost possible to visualize the star-gazer, and to feel his aspiration springing away from his misery. He has far less substance in stanza xiii, the asseverations of which would seem to be reshaped and reduced rather than reinforced by the lines in question.

it may be that in vain
I would essay as I have sung to sing.
Yet, though a dreary strain, to this I cling,
So that it wean me from the weary dream
Of selfish grief or gladness—so it fling
Forgetfulness around me—it shall seem
To me, though to none else, a not ungrateful theme.

The ecstatic retreat from "this world of woe" ("gladness" is a virtual irrelevance for our Childe) follows in stanza v:

. . . Thought seeks refuge in lone caves, yet rife
With *airy images, and shapes* which dwell
Still unimpair'd, though old,
in the soul's haunted cell.
(italics added)

And disillusionment punctually follows; like the naturalist of stanza xiii, the poet with thought can "traverse earth, / Invisible but gazing," but he knows he cannot keep "his spirit to that flight." The sixth stanza concludes on a note of ecstasy. The seventh begins: "Yet I must think less wildly." This acknowledgment—a sort of foretaste of romantic irony in Byron—will not stop him from soaring over and over again, but neither will it cease to be the practical terminus of his ambiguous "flight," with its equal suggestion of achieved exaltation and desperate getting away. The keynote of the new canto, accordingly, should be described as negative, but its tone as changeable or marked by the surface *mobilité* so characteristic of Byron.[7]

[7] It is worth stressing that his *mobilité* is largely symptomatic. Byron's mind appears to have worked by incessant qualifications; more than any of his contemporaries he is given to the use of

The first view of Byron and the first use of Nature, following the preliminary stanza of dedication and stage-setting, appear to establish the controlling terms for the entire canto just as surely as its opening lines do for *The Prelude*. Like Wordsworth, Byron conveys a strong sense of beginning, or at least of resumption, and an equally strong sense of destination wholly in keeping with the concept of pilgrimage:

> Once more upon the waters, yet once more!
> And the waves bound beneath me as a steed
> That knows his rider. Welcome to their roar!
> Swift be their guidance wheresoe'er it lead!
> Though the strain'd mast should quiver as a reed,
> And the rent canvass fluttering strew the gale,
> Still must I on; for I am as a weed,
> Flung from the rock on Ocean's foam to sail
> Where'er the surge may sweep, the tempest's
>   breath prevail.

An atmosphere of confidence as to the destination and exuberance over the new beginning is palpable in these lines. The exclamatory welcome, buoyant terms like "bound" and "swift," the concept of mastery in the image of the steed "that knows his rider," and the implication

---

qualifying connectives such as "but," "still," and "yet." This habit at times becomes manneristic and almost bewildering (see *Childe Harold* i.lxxxii-lxxxiv). It is, however, virtually never a sign of sheer instability, but rather a measure of reluctance to settle prematurely in an intricate field: it is not sufficiently emphasized in criticism that mobility, while it involves a lively response to each new stimulus, does not mean that each new stimulus drives out the previous one(s). It retards definitive conclusions less by changing the mind than by swarming it with variegated data. Byron's scrupulosity has its own honor, and can establish a revealing perspective from which to view the more successful philosophizing of Wordsworth or Shelley.

of ability of cope "wheresoe'er" the waves lead, "where'er"—in heightened, stirring language—"the surge may sweep": all these features make for a light-hearted, if not a light-headed mood. But alas! it is illusion, all.

Take the speaker as "rider" of the waves, for example. The metaphor is audacious as much in what it omits (the unsuitably passive, wooden sailing vessel and its other passengers) as in what it asserts (a cavalier's relationship, in terms of will and force, between a single man and the ocean). And it achieves perfection in its audacity. The physical elements necessary to it as an image remain sparse and sketchy: bounding ocean-as-steed, and rider. But they are as suggestive as they are slight. Their ultimate effect clearly is bound up with the unrepresented, potential sensuousness of the verb "knows" in the crucial clause: "That knows his rider." The image, typically attracting our attention to the sensuous while inviting our apprehension of the abstract, shifts away from the sensuous with the combination of *knowledge* and *steed*. The attribution of knowledge to the ocean-steed—its "bound" *is* regular and progressive, as if responding to a rider—tells us less about it than about *the character* of the rider, who otherwise suffers from a certain vagueness. He is experienced, an expert, a man of action in a world larger and brighter than life (he rides a steed, not a horse), a man of resolution and poise, facing the world openly and securely, responded to spontaneously and generously by that world. But is not the easy richness of the image challenged and ultimately nullified when we learn that the steed controls the rider, that the "guidance" belongs not to the pilgrim but to the waves? Or that the rider of the waves rides "as a weed"? And that his confidence is cockiness born of defiance, since he has been uprooted and dropped on the aimless sea?

For I am as a weed
Flung from the rock [stability]
on Ocean's foam to sail....

If Byron seems as eager for any eventuality as Wordsworth starting *The Prelude,* if he too seems as "free as a
bird" and as ready to follow a "wandering cloud," he is
not prepared like Wordsworth to aver that he "cannot
miss [his] way." Pilgrim or no, he has no way, counting
among the "wanderers o'er Eternity / Whose bark drives
on and on, and anchor'd ne'er shall be" (lxx). The tempered jubilance and centripetal will[8] of the elder poet in
facing a wide-open situation become, in the younger
one, distempered elation and unruliness; a chastened
Byron will properly trim his sails in *Childe Harold* iv,
claiming only to "have laid [his] hand upon [the Ocean's]
mane" (clxxxiv).

Byron's instability is compounded of trauma at being
"flung from the rock"[9] and of the sheer recognition of objective confusion. The difference between him and
Wordsworth is salient in their response to Nature, for
Byron does not so much aspire to Wordsworthian nat-
uralism as he experiments with it in his particular crisis.
In gross terms, Nature's power is understood to be for
Wordsworth an abiding one, aggregative and unified
despite superficial diversity, generous to bestow or, in the

[8] Wordsworth's voice rings out with the glad cry that he is
"free. / Free as a bird," but his is a liberty with its own goal and
discipline; he is free *"to settle"* (*The Prelude* i, 8-9; italics added).
By contrast, as Gleckner suggests, Byron makes "a pilgrimage without faith or shrine" (*Ruins,* p. 230).

[9] Without underestimating the psycho-biographical crisis of 1816
—brilliantly summarized by Robert F. Gleckner (*Ruins,* p. 225)—
I think it possible that Byron found in his unmooring from home
and homeland a terrible material reiteration of that primary
spiritual loss which he already knew as a romantic poet conscious
of time.

crisis of time, to restore the gift of goodness, joy, and peace. Nature is purposive and educating, bringing man by due stages, in due season to know and appreciate his gifted place. She is philanthropic, and leads "to love of Man." Material Nature expresses the spiritual; she works with man's Imagination to reveal the intrinsically spiritual quality of the universe.

For Byron the force of Nature proves random and contingent, as likely to expose human weakness as to buttress it, as likely to be otiose as effectual. Nature turns into a very model of randomness in the key second stanza of *Childe Harold* iii, where wave, and surge, weed, foam, and wind declare the universality of movement and suggest the brute compulsion to move that the speaker confesses ("Still must I on"). To read one stanza (xlv) of this canto with the Mt. Snowdon episode in mind is to see vividly the separation of Byron and Wordsworth. Byron has a man ascending, but he is *any* man in a general situation, not Wordsworth's particular man in a representative situation. From this point the differences multiply. Byron writes:

> He who ascends to mountain-tops, shall find
> The loftiest peaks most wrapt in clouds and snow;
> He who surpasses or subdues mankind,
> Must look down on the hate of those below.
> Though high *above* the sun of glory glow,
> And far *beneath* the earth and ocean spread,
> *Round* him are icy rocks, and loudly blow
> Contending tempests on his naked head,
> And thus reward the toils which to those summits led.

Byron here offers the Wordsworthian panorama, the heavens, the mountain, the earth and ocean being em-

braced in one picture. But Wordsworth's picture of continuity and ultimate unity has been changed into one
of radical division. The man who "ascends to mountain-
tops" has been cut off from mankind, and cannot reach
the sun on the other side. His relation to both is negative:
hostility between him and the rest of men, aeons of futility between him and the sun, as the author's emphasis
on the adverb *above* and the encompassment with icy
rocks attest. And, perhaps the cardinal thing to observe,
the mountain scene functions as metaphor for Byron,
while for Wordsworth it is at once reality and symbol.
Byron uses Nature, as it were, optionally to add impact
to what he is saying about man's relation to man and to
the universe. Wordsworth is talking about Nature *as
well as* about man's mind and his position in the universe; one is necessary to the other.

It would seem that, from Byron's perspective, nothing
is *necessary* about Nature. The "majestic Rhine," passive,
almost pictorial as a "blending of all beauties" (iii.xlvi),
takes on intrinsic life and virtue as Byron personifies it:
"exulting and abounding river! Making thy waves a
blessing" (1). But what is its efficacy? As an agent of
"Maternal Nature" (xlvi), does it constitute an essential
power?

The structure of the Rhine stanzas offers the answer.
These stanzas are pressed inside a wave-like statement
of function and limitation, of aspiration and implied
negation. As they begin we are told that "true Wisdom's
world will be / Within its own creation, *or* in thine, /
Maternal Nature!" (italics added). Shortly, we see Nature not merely as an alternative force but as a deficient
and frustrated one. The beauty of the banks of the Rhine

would endure forever
Could man but leave thy [the Rhine's] bright creation so,
Nor its fair promise from the surface mow
With the sharp scythe of conflict,—then to see
Thy valley of sweet waters, were to know
Earth paved like Heaven; and to seem such to me
Even now what wants thy stream?—
                that it should Lethe be.
    (l; italics added)

The course of the Rhine, almost made to fuse with the course of time, can wash away physical harm, or at least the evidence of it; spiritual harm it is powerless to affect:

A thousand battles have assail'd thy banks,
But these and half their fame have pass'd away.
And Slaughter heap'd on high his weltering ranks;
Their very graves are gone, and what are they?
Thy tide wash'd down the blood of yesterday,
And all was stainless, and on thy clear stream
Glass'd with its dancing light the sunny ray;
But o'er the blacken'd memory's blighting dream
Thy waves would vainly roll, all sweeping
                   as they seem.
    (li)

Rounding out the pattern, this anti-Wordsworthian thwarting of Nature by memory is involved again in the farewell stanza to the Rhine (lix) with its mournful subjunctive cast. Significantly, too, it has been anticipated in the peerless vignette on the Battle of Waterloo, where wide human compassion and not a private disease of conscience, where the very structure of human existence and not a deformed personality inhibits the "contrivings" of Nature, and betray their futility (iii.xxx).

Nor should the song, "The castled crag of Drachenfels," which is set into the Rhine stanzas, be left out of account. For the song, with its couplet refrain insistently revising and qualifying the high estimate of Nature in the first eight lines of each stanza, prefers "one [woman's] soft breast" to the "breast of waters," or at least finds Nature and the pastoral *mise-en-scène* wanting because that person is not present to share the moment. If the Rhine "wanted" or lacked a Lethean power before, its banks now "want" one thing, "Thy gentle hand to clasp in mine!" The speaker makes the woman the essential and paramount element in this projected perfection:

> Nor could on earth a spot be found
> To nature and to me so dear,
> Could thy dear eyes in following mine
> Still sweeten more these banks of Rhine!

The song, typically enough, treats Nature as a hebdomadal instead of an essential experience, and in fact could stand as a high-toned precedent for the consummate tourist-post-card message: "Wish you were here." M. K. Joseph's sense that on one level all of Canto III tends to be "a versified travel-journal" gets strong support here (*Byron the Poet*, p. 71).[10] Indeed Byron turns to his next scene, his next tableau, almost casually: "But these [the banks of the Rhine] recede." One has little sense of his carrying the Rhine in imagination as he goes on to the Alps, making or finding each experience a part of *one* experience. It is extremely difficult, then, to take the palinodic, post-farewell stanzas to the Rhine (lx-lxi)

---

[10] In the "short journal of each day's progress" kept for his "Sister Augusta," Byron comments favorably on scenery and song, and adds: "Dearest [Augusta], you do not know how I should have liked this, were you with me" (*LJ*, III, 349, 361).

at face value. Byron declares that "there can be no farewell to scene like thine; / The mind is colour'd by thy
every hue." One simply sees nothing in the poem to uphold this kind of declaration, especially in the face of the
adverse evidence built up through the previous one
hundred and sixty-six lines. The palinode is positively
impressive out of context; in context it turns out to be,
like the earlier utterance of natural faith in stanza xiii,
neither fitting nor quite plausible.

The tortuous stanzas on Lake Leman that conclude
the new canto contain at least three forthright professions of positive faith in or identification with Nature or
with Love, which is patently at home and flourishing in
Nature (st. civ). But these transcendental professions
(st. lxxii, lxxxv-xci, c-civ) in my judgment stand to the
whole canto as the palinode to the stanzas on the Rhine.
In stanza lxii, for example, Byron writes of the Alps:

> All that expands the spirit, yet appals,
> Gather around these summits, as to show
> How Earth may pierce to Heaven,
>   yet leave vain man below.

Twenty stanzas later he declares that "the soul can
flee, / And with the sky, the peak, the heaving plain /
Of ocean, or the stars, mingle, and not in vain." Between
these opposite positions no movement of reconciliation
develops in the poem. The basis of a new choice is not a
new belief, but a renewed need to believe arising from
the failure of the previous belief. As Leslie A. Marchand
says in his introduction to *Selected Poetry of Lord
Byron*, the poet "occasionally, from the depths of disillusionment, . . . turns in sheer exhaustion to a kind of

tranquillity."[11] By the same token, he sometimes erupts with the surplus store of energy which tranquillity may produce. But the opposite positions do not fail to affect each other, so that one discerns, even in the final yea-saying phase of the canto, a curious swinging between positive assertion and rhetorical questions which have a markedly tentative, even dubious ring (lxix-lxxv). Byron seems to be asking for reassurance, to be trying to reason himself into transcendentalism, and with a process of thought something less than impeccable. "The race of life" in a "contentious world," he tells us, will always be "a hopeless flight" (lxix-lxx). "Is it not better, *then*, to be alone?" (lxxi, italics added). Though this far from necessary conclusion be granted, it does not form any sort of basis for the ensuing declaration: "I live not in myself, but I become / Portion of that around me; and to me / High mountains are a feeling. . . ." For, as Arnold reminds us in *Empedocles on Etna*, being weary does not prove that man has where to rest. The turbulent, even protean quality of the canto persists in these stanzas: they earn somewhat less than they claim philosophically, and one is not surprised to see Byron shut them down, as he has shut down the stanzas on the Rhine, with a brusque remark: "But this is not my theme" (lxxvi).

The difference I have suggested between an abstract acknowledgement of Nature and a vital faith in her powers is clearly reflected in the difference between what Byron says of Clarens in prose and what he writes in *Childe Harold* iii. In a personal note appended to the apostrophe: "Clarens, sweet Clarens, birthplace of deep Love!", Byron celebrates "its peculiar adaptation to the

[11] (New York, 1951), p. x.

persons and events with which it has been peopled."
But the real quality and value of the place, as he sees it,
goes beyond such associations:

> The feeling with which all around Clarens, and the
> opposite rocks of Meillerie, is invested, is of a still
> higher and more comprehensive order . . . ; it is a
> sense of the existence of love in its most extended
> and sublime capacity, and of our own participa-
> tion of its good and of its glory: it is the great
> principle of the universe, which is there more
> condensed, but not less manifested. . . . If Rous-
> seau had never written, nor lived, the same
> associations would not less have belonged to
> such scenes. . . . He has shown his sense of their
> beauty . . . ; but they have done that for him
> which no human being could do for them.

This "sense" is not translated into *Childe Harold* III
without corruption, even contradiction. The glorified picture of Clarens is tinged with pessimism, with the usual
Byronic "sense" that Love has been "driven" or banished
to a hinterland, and has no place in the world (with this
further inference, it seems, that since Love must either
"advance or die," decay or grow, it is now decaying and
dying). Furthermore, the suggestion that Heaven could
only "deign" to smile "On man and man's research," and
the final statement, in connection with Clarens, of human incertitude (cviii) materially diminish the force,
perhaps the very plausibility of the opening claims for
Love.

The degree of interest which must be accorded Byron's
statements on Nature for themselves should not be allowed to dim the fact that he is not dealing with Nature

in or for itself: Nature is not his theme. Nor does the
canto strictly speaking hold out a theme. Rather it
essays possibilities in a discontinuous scheme of self-
assertion and self-cancellation. And Nature is not one
possibility but a catchall term for an assortment of possibilities which besides clashing together also clash with
yet other possibilities, such as personal love or family
love, art or empire. Still the things to which Byron resorts for sanctuary and assurance prove futile only sec-
ondarily because they clash and destroy one another;
futility inheres in their status as resorts, as momentary
conveniences of a mind no more capable of all-compos-
ing resolution than of quieting compromise. What Byron
wants and needs is nowhere more salient than in the
opening address to his daughter; it would seem a fitting
perversity that while the poem has an incontestable show
of symmetry and order in the concluding return of attention to that daughter, the latter lines actually an-
nounce a state of loss and abandonment. The framing
stanzas on the daughter, if anything, provide a steady,
wide focus on the typical syndrome of hope, reflection,
and chagrin.[12]

[12] William H. Marshall has done a close structural analysis of
Canto III (*The Structure of Byron's Major Poems*, Philadelphia,
Pa., 1962, pp. 72-81), with results appreciably different from
mine. The recognition that it is fruitful and necessary to deal with
Byron's seemingly ebullient poetry in this way must rank above
any other consideration here, and it is with a sense of loyal reservation that one would wish, at this point above all in *The Structure*,
for a discrimination of the more tenuous and ingenious parallels
in Marshall's plan from the more substantive ones, for an ex-
plication of the nature and features of each parallel, and for a
critical confrontation of the meaning of the rather Homeric
schematization to the canto, which Marshall actually acknowledges
to be lacking even the limited "degree of cohesiveness found in the
monologues and certain other poems of the later periods" (p. 72).
The response of Andrew Rutherford to *Childe Harold* III also calls

The intractable problem for Byron in *Childe Harold* III may be identified as one of inclusivity, or, from a technical standpoint, of continuity. While he shows here his special propensity to entertain divers points of view, he has apparently lost the art of reconciliation seen in "To Edward Noel Long, Esq.," and is not yet adroit enough for the paradoxical art of maintaining them equally. That will emerge most graphically in *Don Juan*. Nor does he, though he seems to think of travel as at once physical and metaphysical—"we may resume / The march of our existence" he writes (st. xcviii)—manage to keep the predictable temporal and geographical gaps of the march from repeating themselves in the area of existence, where continuity and unity would be expected.

The root of the problem, unmistakably, is to be found in the natural failure of Byron's attempt to reason or else to will his way to transcendence. Late in *Childe Harold* III he expresses the belief "that there may be / Words which are things . . ." (cxiv). In the preceding stanzas he seems to fall prey to a perverse, pseudo-realistic interpretation of this statement, to wit, that words create reality in and of themselves, in defiance of what George Santayana calls "existence."[13] Byron implicitly repudiates

for consideration here. Rutherford begins with the thesis that the canto is unified around the "poet-hero's personality and interests," with "four major themes"—the speaker's "own wrongs and sorrows, the fate of genius, the liberty of peoples, the value and significance of Nature"—operating in mutual relation and "imposing a coherence on [the] multitude of observations and reflexions." But this "first favourable impression," far from being borne out, undergoes immediate modification, and the thesis of a formal or schematic unity is tacitly given over (*Byron: A Critical Study*, Stanford, Calif., 1962, pp. 51ff.).

[13] *Scepticism and Animal Faith: Introduction to a System of Philosophy*, New York, 1923, p. 47.

such an attitude in the "Epistle to Augusta," where to recognize the transcendental possibilities in Nature is a far cry from realizing them. If, in his particolored way, he appears to canonize the pseudo-realistic view in *Manfred*, there at least the indomitable mind gets fullest play and the agency of Nature enters by and large negatively into the case.

In theory, especially considering what he had himself done in the mystical way, and also considering the conjunction of his favorable pre-disposition and Shelley's promptings, there might easily have been a renewal of fervor for Byron in 1816. Perhaps, though, a forecast of his failure is latent in "To Edward Noel Long, Esq.," his most accomplished transcendental piece. An arresting and, I think, revealing pattern develops from a comparison of the alter ego figures in this poem, "Tintern Abbey," and "Frost at Midnight": in order, the poet's contemporary, his somewhat younger sister, and his infant son.

Wordsworth's experience, so far as it has been recapitulated in Dorothy's existence, obtains a confirmation and, more important yet, a continuation *ad perpetuitatem*. What he has undergone, what she is undergoing, may be taken as typical, as a manifestation of an abstract principle. Wordsworth discloses Dorothy's future just as surely as she embodies his past, incarnates his memory: *sum quod eris*, he can say, *fui quod es*. They meet in a present that is not uniform but subtly adapted to their distinct circumstances. The process of time provides assurance of eternity.

Neither Coleridge nor Byron fully matches Wordsworth's stably progressive continuum of past-present-future. The enlarged gap between Coleridge and Hartley's ages, their *states*, gets reflection in the difference

between their environments ("Frost at Midnight," 11.48-
64), and comes to symbolize a basic difference between
Wordsworth and Coleridge. For, though Coleridge is no
less confident of Hartley's future than Wordsworth of
Dorothy's, Hartley continues his father's hopes, not his
experience. Coleridge has not had Wordsworth's past;
Hartley's future was once his own, when he kept watch-
ing the classroom door with unabating excitement and
hope. In other words, Coleridge faithfully, *wishfully*
projects the future of which Wordsworth tenders solid
earnests and for which, so to speak, he provides. Byron,
using his colleague Long, builds up a past-present as
sure and subtle as Wordsworth's, but offers not even
Coleridge's wish for the future.

Two separate versions of a potential future can validly
be discerned in *Childe Harold* III. Ada represents one
of them. She compares readily with Coleridge's Hartley,
but the future she means to Byron is seriously damaged
by circumstances, and the shattered family relationship
finally images itself in the philosophical one. Augusta
Leigh, in turn, bears comparison with Wordsworth's
Dorothy, uncannily so when Byron associates her with
gentleness and serenity in Nature:

> once I loved
> Torn ocean's roar, but thy [Lake Leman]
> soft murmuring
> Sounds sweet as if a Sister's voice reproved,
> That I with stern delights should e'er
> have been so moved.
>
> (lxxxv)

Again, though, biography gets in the way of philosophy,
or rather, biography is not moulded into philosophy.
Augusta confirms Byron in his isolation rather than help-

ing him to see comprehensively either in the dimension of Nature or in the dimension of Time. It is evident that even the superiority to turbulence and flux implied in the quoted verses involves a mood, not a state. In his usual bursting, centrifugal way, he turns in the superiority of peace and identification with "clear, placid Leman" for the superiority of force and identification—typically wishful—with "Lightning" (xcii-xcvii).

The plethora of *distinct* proposals for self-redemption in *Childe Harold* III threatens each with extinction. In other words, Ada does not fail Byron as an agent of reconciliation and hope because of domestic acrimonies, or only because of them (Coleridge is not known to have been overjoyed with his marriage); she fails because Byron keeps "busily seeking, with a continual change," hectically taxing his susceptibilities and his means to redemption. Nature's physical dominance of the scene makes its status little different from Ada's. For Nature is itself made up of elements basically in conflict with one another. The various aspects of Nature that thrive in *Childe Harold* III (serenity and violence, say) thrive at one another's expense.

What survives the natural competition, what Byron sees fittest to preserve amounts to a distillation from each of the episodes of possible redemption, in which the characteristic action has taken the form of absorption, either of Byron himself into something other, or of something other into himself. That self, remarkably unstable in its variety, yet has proven more tenacious than its saviors. It persists, they arise and fall away; and so in retrospect a new emphasis develops, for Byron and the reader alike, an emphasis summed up in Rutherford's judgment that "the central interest is always in the poet-hero himself" (*Byron: A Critical Study*, p. 63), rather than with the things outside and around him. Their variety, in a profound way, answers and subsists on its versatility, for it includes and demands them all, and exhausts them all, making them, even where they are needed, topical. They are contingent, it has proven viable, substantive. Or, to put it another way, the self with its incurable agitations and aspirations does not, having made its ineffectual pilgrimage to shrines in and out of Nature, simply end where it began. The world of expectations has undergone a change, and a critical shift in emphasis has been imposed: the self which has turned for succor in reality and not just in "symbolic projection,"[14] to things without, must turn to itself. This shift fosters a new sense of proportion and value, for if it can be desperate to be, as it were, alienated and unanchored,[15] it can be a source of muted, even somber gladness for advocates of "a firm will, and a deep sense, / Which even in torture can descry / Its own concenter'd recompense, / Triumphant when it dares defy . . ." ("Prometheus," ll.55-58). The viability of triumphant defiance was to be put to the proof by Byron, with such enthusiasm and eloquence that we see fit to call it Byronic. It is complexly so; Byron's habit of plural consciousness holds even where defiance seems purest, and defiance takes its place as an episode, an experiment in the Byronic vein.

[14] Edward L. Bostetter, *The Romantic Ventriloquists*, Seattle, 1963, p. 268. It seems to me that even when he threatens, or aspires to "embody and unbosom" himself in "Lightning" (st. xcvii), Byron is trying to adopt something from outside to give definition to an essential if strenuous obscurity within.

[15] Scott, in a letter to J.B.S. Morritt, expressed the doubt whether "human nature can support the constant working of an imagination so dark and so strong" (quoted by Ian Jack, *English Literature: 1815-1832*, being Vol. x of *The Oxford History of English Literature*, ed. F. P. Wilson and Bonamy Dobrée, Oxford, 1963).

· III ·

THE FATAL BOUNDS
OF THE WILL
The facts will promptly blunt his ardor.—STATIUS

Critical theorists celebrate as one of the outstanding marks of romanticism the realization that the seat of value is in the self, and the obligation of the self the apprehension of its home beyond brute circumstances of time and place; its "heart and home," as Wordsworth declares, "is with infinitude." A decisive shift in orientation takes place here. For where traditional Christianity had promised redemption of the individual from eternal wretchedness by a briefly incarnate Christ, Agent of Infinitude, romanticism is seen propounding a redemption of infinitude from entrenched materialism by the self, Bearer of Infinitude—so that Christ, as used by Blake for example, comes to represent man-as-God more truly than God-as-man. It would appear quite fitting, then, for Byron to have been brought home to himself in 1816, just as it would appear standard for him, in the name of that self, to have laid claim to infinitude. But Byron's situation and his response admit of features that have no exact parallel within the romantic complex.

The cardinal quality that sets Byron's presentation of the self apart in its time I would describe as starkness. The frustrating interaction of circumstances and personality which almost systematically in *Childe Harold* III strips the self of armor, integument, and salve leads to a minor metaphysical insight in Byron's work, in the implicit recognition that self-assertion counts more than self-regulation in a difficult universe. Of course one cannot be blind to moments of starkness undergone by the other great romantics: as when Keats finds himself tolled back from the nightingale, the blessed world of vision, to his "*sole* self"; or when Wordsworth experiences "a sense, / Death-like, of treacherous desertion . . . / In the last place of refuge—[his] own soul"; or in Coleridge's "Dejection: An Ode" or in certain of Blake's *Songs of Experience* or *Europe: A Prophecy*. But these instances only remind one that the romantic poet's affirmation of the Self Infinite is rarely divorced from the context, if not the formal process, of argument. It bears emphasizing that the inevitable recoil of romantic self-concern is the recognition of the way others will stand as strangers to one's own presuppositions and predilections, and the recoil of romantic vision the awareness of profane, even antagonistic views. An undernote of philosophical differing, of necessary, if muted argument continually impinges on the reader's consciousness in the most affirmative romantic poetry; but not as a distraction. Rather it leads attention unresisting back to the main theme with little further need for a suspension of disbelief. There has been a barely audible clashing and getting done with the adversary mind, such as we may perceive when Wordsworth writes: "And I must think, do all I can, / That there was pleasure there." The interpolated phrase "do all I can," acknowledges opposition which is obviously made futile (I *must* think). Wordsworth's claim to vision, and by the same token, the claims *of* his vision have to be made good against the possibility of error. "If this be but a vain belief . . ." he worries in "Tintern Abbey," and goes on to purge himself and his reader alike of such misgivings, the force of his renewed conviction breaking the grammatical pattern with an anacoluthon:

> ... yet oh! how oft—
> In darkness and amidst the many shapes
> Of joyless daylight; when the fretful stir
> Unprofitable, and the fever of the world,
> Have hung upon the beatings of my heart—
> How oft, in spirit, have I turned to thee,
> O sylvan Wye! thou wanderer thro' the woods,
> How often has my spirit turned to thee!

His doubt, played out on a rationalistic, argumentative speculation, shows itself to be unsupportable in the real order of fact and faith. The moment of argument becomes a foil to the moment of affirmation as the verse paragraph swells with exclamations and nearly ritual repetition ("often" works in diction *and* in experience) to annihilate the potentially crippling doubt with which it commences. The doubt, not the belief, is vain. Yet the element of doubt, the possibility of negation appears in a way necessary to the visionary affirmations of romantic poetry. To recognize the immortality of the bird's voice in "Ode to a Nightingale" or "To a Skylark" or "To the Cuckoo" is also inevitably to recall mortality. And to express immortality is impossible except through denial, or suspension, or actual time and transitoriness. These latter must keep a half-life in the mind for the very sake of one's belief in immortality. The visionary poet thus with equal validity enjoys, or has hopes of, or only continues to believe in, vision. His poetry may be a matter of pursuit as well as of possession, and need do no more than set itself positively on the spiral of aspiration.

This dualistic idea of aspiration and relationship, the

concept of ex-stasis that is bound up with the romantic portrayal of the Self, Byron brings to its lowest pitch. The possibility of negation gets in him the kind of substance that represses aspiration into unbending defiance, replacing identification in, and with, the Universe with general self-assertion. It is a rhetorical emblem of a metaphysical orientation that Byron has no nightingale or urn, no cuckoo or solitary reaper, no skylark or west wind, no mountain and no light with which he can collaborate in the discovery and perpetuation of value. At least, not in 1816. He has his special passages of passion, of symbolism, of action, but these eliminate more than they create, building up, as it were, to nakedness. As in *Childe Harold* III they create the image of a man unaccommodated though unlamenting, undefended and yet not reduced to defeat. In *Manfred* that figure is again presented, and for the first time substantially characterized.

The profile of unaccommodated man, as critics have perennially remarked, has another and doubtless more spectacular side from which Manfred appears as unaccommodating man—defiant, seemingly solipsistic, and in less danger of being possessed than self-possessed. But Manfred develops into something more than an all-repudiating hero. He crackles with an aggrieved superiority, but actually by this enables us to observe that the fierceness of his rejection of whatever he has or is offered corresponds to the depth of his fixation on what is, more than coincidentally, unattainable. He typifies the perfectionist and iconoclast in collision with reality, and ordained to recover strength and sanity through acceptance rather than action and aggression.

Notwithstanding Manfred's apparent energy and self-involvement, the play is moving toward an ideal of acceptance from the start. Thus Manfred early implies a repudiation of his past deeds, or misdeeds; "I have ceased / To justify my deeds unto myself— / The last infirmity of evil" (i.ii.27-29). It is worth stressing that Manfred becomes a hero less for what he can do than for what he can do without. A major rhythm is established in the play with his rejection of an assortment of orthodox forces and relationships. His opening speech—and the first words of the drama—straightway engages us in the mystique of doing without. It recapitulates the things ("Philosophy and science," etc.) which have "avail'd not" for him, presenting him as the disengaged man:

> I have no dread,
> And feel the curse to have no natural fear,
> Nor fluttering throb, that beats with hope or wishes,
> Or lurking love of something on the earth.

What he does have is a purpose ("Now to my task") or, to put it more abstractly, a will. That will must seem curiously thwarted if compared with the will of a Tamburlaine: Manfred fails to achieve anything, and even puts aside such particular goals as knowledge, benevolence, conquest, and happiness. His will goes practically unsatisfied. But Byron's play, concerned with a different order of will than Marlowe's, plants its standard on a different peak. Tamburlaine triumphs over all obstacles and opposition, only succumbing to death; Manfred defies all dangers and powers, including death. The emphasis in *Tamburlaine* falls primarily on material operations, in Manfred on a spiritual condition, so that the creature's death experienced in common by the two heroes becomes for one a reversal, for the other a culmination of his career. Manfred, as a hero who excels by doing without, proves in his most perfect moment capable of the ultimate excellence of doing without life.

It is crucial to see that Manfred rises above the things he rejects,[1] and at the same time to see that in this he only achieves a negative victory, indicating what he is too strong to submit to, not what he is strong enough to realize. And the latter does not depend on an exercise of will. Manfred's ultimate state takes him clearly beyond mere strength of denial, or of assertion, beyond what Shelley calls "the anarchy / Of hopes and fears." The drama itself seems so far from centering around the manifestations of a substantive will that no other character evinces even Manfred's passing and partial reliance on will, whereas the will of Tamburlaine for example gets its basic definition by out-towering the stilted will of others.

The early spectacle of Manfred's emphatically self-conscious and self-confessing determination too easily seduces attention from the fact that he is met in a pattern of self-discovery and self-acceptance, just as his outbursts of pride tend to drown out a steady note of eagerness for reconciliation and calm. This needs to be remembered in judging his relationship with the rest of the characters; his haughty rejection of them, seemingly progressive in its sequence from Chamois Hunter to Abbot to otherworld Spirits, actually serves to show him arrested at a point of psychological and spiritual crisis; he is living in the trap which the Stranger so dispassionately sets for Arnold in *The Deformed Transformed*,

---

[1] The case for Manfred, the triumphant, is substantially presented by Samuel C. Chew in the relevant chapter of *The Dramas of Lord Byron*, Baltimore, Maryland, 1915.

with "no bond / But [his] own will, no contract save
[his] own deeds" (Pt. i, i.150-151). These widely differing figures, however, are not the ciphers they are often
taken for; they show us a sort of abortive excellence in
Manfred, and help to define the impasse of Manfred's
situation.

On the cliffs of the Jungfrau and in the mountain cot-
tage, at the outset of the drama, Manfred is seen in a
natural and human context. He is divorcing himself from
both, finding nature's beauty and man's compassion alike
irrelevant and impotent for himself. But he leaves his
impress behind. The Chamois Hunter defers to him as a
superior man, and he signalizes Manfred's spirit rather
than his agility in saying that the latter,

> Who seems not of my trade, . . . yet hath reach'd
> A height which none even of our mountaineers,
> Save our best hunters, may attain.
>   (i.ii.60-62)

Untouched by the world he is leaving, Manfred is also
untouched by the underworld he dares to enter. He dis-
dains the shock and indignation of the attendant Spirits
in the Hall of Arimanes (iii.iv), and indeed extracts from
them the same simultaneously personal and professional
praise the Chamois Hunter has accorded him, as one of
the Spirits breathlessly recognizes in him a "Magian of
great power, and fearful skill." There is, finally, the world
that comes to Manfred, in the person of the Abbot of St.
Maurice who, working in the human sphere in the interest of a spiritual, divine order, in himself comprehends
features of two worlds. The indefatigable Abbot shares
the experience of the Chamois Hunter and the chthonian
Spirits; he can do nothing with Manfred, but finds some-

thing admirable and attractive in him, sensing qualities that normally enable one to take a fair place among the brotherhood of man and, ultimately, the communion of saints (II.i). The degree of Manfred's excellence, as well as the degree of his separateness can be discerned in the subjunctive with which Hunter, Abbott, and Spirit all express their responses to him: "You should have been a hunter," "This should have been a noble creature," "He would have made / An awful spirit." The range of his influence can be gauged by the way he moves representatives of the secular, the religious, and the chthonian orders.

Yet it is all too evident that his impregnable loftiness hinges on a secret defect. Certainly there are points at which the "noble" and "awful" uniqueness of Manfred presents itself in a dubious light. In the guilty action with Astarte which Manuel speaks of to the Abbot *offstage*, and which Byron coyly drags in without unwrapping, Manfred has without doubt been the aggressive, the demanding, the reckless party. He is thus liable to the charge of selfishness, and his conduct after realizing that he has in effect victimized Astarte by inducing her into a passing act of passion contrary to her profoundest principles turns his supposed individualism into something more like peevishness. He repudiates philosophy, altruism and so on (I.i) because he has failed to maintain "a kind of transcendental state outside ordinary human experience, . . . an ineffable absolute irreconcilable with the world, . . . [and] *more real than the world*."[2] He does it impressively, philosophically even, with *sententiae* like "Sorrow is knowledge," and "The Tree of Knowledge is

[2] Denis de Rougemont, *Love in the Western World*, trans. Montgomery Belgion, rev. and augmented edn., New York, 1956, p. 39.

not that of Life," but it remains tantamount to striking out at others to beguile personal pain.

The emphasis in the early scenes of the play on Manfred's will and what it can make others do tends to corroborate this judgment. Manfred, with the Seven Spirits, and on the Mountain of the Jungfrau, seeks to prescribe terms to the Universe, seeks to act and be immune to consequences. Even his implied yearning toward "serenity of soul," which he recognizes as a form of "immortality" (ii.ii), betrays a known imperfection in his individualism. The root conflict of the drama occurs inside Manfred's mind, and is but intimated in the more conspicuous confrontations with Chamois Hunter or Abbot or otherworld agents. Its root issue has finally two distinguishable terms to be resolved: can Manfred keep from losing himself to various outside forces, can he withstand the "temptation" to "the abandonment of his will"?[3] And if so, can he further find for himself, instead of deadened detachment, a more than mortal "serenity"?

In a sense, the play drives Manfred toward the fullest experience of his somewhat irritable boast that he is, like the lion, "alone"; his metaphor expresses life's literal truth, and life's uncompromising challenge. His difficulties with truth and challenge alike arise chiefly out of his relation to Astarte, whose universe he has not expanded but shattered in pressing her toward some uncanonized transaction. Manfred must learn to *accept*, albeit without sacrificing his essential self; and he must learn not to *expect*, and this is a lesson that he takes longest to learn where Astarte is concerned. His intensest expectation, and gravest weakness, appears as he presses her, or her Phantom, for an expression of forgiveness,

[3] Elton, A *Survey*, ii, 164.

then of love, at the end of Act II. He is denied, and as one of the Spirits present vindictively observes, "He is convulsed—This is to be a mortal / And seek the things beyond mortality." But what looks like the final humbling for Manfred is only the sign of a crisis, in dramatic as well as spiritual terms. Manfred responds superbly. Another Spirit reports on the scene:

> Yet, see, he mastereth himself, and makes
> His torture tributary to his will.

These lines, perhaps, tend to revive the idea of Manfred's predominance of will. In fact, what gets "mastered" here is the curl of the interested self; the will works as a rectified will, not aiming toward (or away from) objects, but purely sustaining the integrity of the existential self. The present "tributary" does not swell the hero's store, or consciousness of will. If anything it destroys it. Manfred emerges from the scene purged of the defects which had led him into it. He remains alert and involved, but he is no longer harshly purposive; in his brief exchange with Nemesis as the scene and act come to a close he shows himself above all ready for whatever may arise. Significantly Astarte now virtually disappears from the play, and Manfred enjoys a new state:

> There is a calm upon me—
> Inexplicable stillness! which till now
> Did not belong to what I knew of life.
> (III.i)

Here Manfred attains a dignity beyond what merely "lies in his conscious awareness of, and defiance of, the

THE FATAL BOUNDS OF THE WILL

fates which are his antagonists."[4] The serenity for which he has yearned has in effect befallen him, and that in the unlikeliest of places, where he has been thrust through the final gate of agitation.

Clearly this experience of serenity on the part of the "mortal" affords the immortality which he had expected of it, inasmuch as it frees him from the sense of incompleteness and instability inherent in mortality; it is the Emersonian idea of immortality as being "not length of life, but depth of life, . . . not duration, but a taking of the soul out of time." We may note, too, that the singular experience of immortality is given a universal moral bearing in Manfred's identification of it as "the golden secret, the sought 'Kalon.'" He has discovered mankind's "good," not just his own; and he has discovered it neither in enormous energy nor in vacant self-forgetfulness, but in the strength of vital peace. And where before he has been bent on rejecting or destroying all terms of existence, his new state proves harmonious and inclusive. It brings back the scholar in him, for one thing, and we may find in his recollection of his "tablets" a noteworthy echo of Hamlet, in an affirmative chord befitting one to whom has been revealed not evil but unprophesied grace:

> It hath enlarged my thoughts with a new sense,
> And I within my tablets would note down
> That there is such a feeling.

Manfred's feeling, his knowledge of spiritual goodness and self-accord opposes as it also redeems his earlier condition of desperate stagnancy, which even he rec-

[4] Peter L. Thorslev, "Freedom and Destiny: Romantic Contraries," *Bucknell Review*, XIV (May 1966), 44.

ognized as a "curse." If his "pride and defiance" have any "moral-philosophic value" (Rutherford, p. 91), it must be the negative one of constituting symptoms of a soul dis-eased, of representing the problem rather than the foundation of the play. Manfred's "Promethean" ability to withstand various orthodox and systematic attacks on his self-possession should finally be taken as ambiguous, being but a half-way stage between the ultimate degradation of surrender and his ultimate attainment of a more than personal "calm of mind, all passion spent." For while it could seem that Manfred ceases "to struggle toward resolution,"[5] in actuality resolution has befallen him. He knows what it means "wenn ein Glückliches fällt."

Two other problematical points are resolved less successfully as regards Manfred's character. The first is the relation of Manfred to the Abbot, who, unlike the Chamois Hunter and the assorted servants and Spirits parading through the play, ends up in the final version of the play as much more than a foil to the hero. He is a considerable character in his own right, and his position carries substantial weight; because of him *Manfred* escapes being "a one-character drama."[6] Manfred, rejecting his aid, is far from negating his values. Ultimately he fails to break out of the orbit of his priestly function, as he does out of the orbit of the Chamois Hunter and Astarte. The Abbot is present and active to the end, and his persistence, without arrogance or prurience as it is, adds at once to his credit as a priest and to his stature as a character. This is not to gloss over the fact that he is practically stymied. He has, and can have, no proper

[5] Marshall, *The Structure of Byron's Major Poems*, p. 23.
[6] *Ibid.*, p. 97.

answer to the serene and simple finality of Manfred's expiring words: "Old man! 't is not so difficult to die." But the play allows him the concluding statement:

He's gone, his soul hath ta'en its earthless flight; Whither? I dread to think; but he is gone.

In this way Byron himself has partially "destroyed the whole effect and moral" of the drama (*LJ*, IV, 157). Manfred avoids the merely conventional piety of Maturin's Bertram: "Lift up your holy hands in charity"; but a problem remains. Has Manfred transcended, or only ignored the possibility intimated in the Abbot's summary? Hasn't the "noble" and "awful" resolution of his last words—the "serenity" which we have been invited to take as a form of "immortality"—been impugned by the fact that the Abbot has the last word? Or do we interpret it that the Abbot retains enough of the intellectual obtuseness and institutional rigidity of the original version to prevent him from appreciating a new existential sanctity in the hero?

Manfred ends on an ambiguous note of affirmation and uncertainty. That uncertainty, however, does not concern the power of the will, which is at best irascible and negative. It concerns the possibility and efficacy of purging the will,[7] and constitutes the final problem to be recognized in the play. Is the hero's philosophy ulti-

---

[7] *Sardanapalus* furnishes an interesting comment on the involutions of the problem of purging the will. The protagonist, making "indulgence" rather than triumph his home belief, only seems purged of the military and dynastic will of his forbears and his enemies. His pleasure-loving pacifism involves a species of urbane individualism, and is converted with revealing speed into martial terms at the point of ultimate danger. The suicide of Sardanapalus, even apart from its ostentation, generates the same misgivings as does that of Addison's Cato, smacking as much of egotistical chagrin as of unworldly self-abnegation.

mately viable? Is his conscience respectable, his character plausible? Even with the affirmative force of "earthless flight" to temper the Abbot's misgivings, the play offers nothing like an answer to such questions, which indeed it raises at the eleventh hour. But as the figure of the self-subsistent hero, most powerfully limned in Manfred, reappears in Byron's work, so does the element of doubt as to his ultimate status.[8] More than this, doubt seems to get amplified into disapprobation as Byron gets closer to the terms of actuality and, in particular, to the contemporary European scene.

In *Cain*, published four years after *Manfred*, the hero is more intimately involved in practical affairs, and therefore more open, or vulnerable, to the turn of events and consequences. Cain is far less experienced than Manfred (the latter inherits a world which the former unwittingly helped to make). He does not object to a life that has somehow failed him, but to the fundamental terms of life, to his given creaturely state. He is, as Marshall points out,[9] closer than Manfred to the problem of right versus wrong, of duty versus egotism, of good versus evil. He is

[8] With a change of environment this represents a revival of the prevailing attitude of the Oriental Tales, where the heroes, whom Jeffrey summarily accused of "voluptuousness" and "misanthropy," do carefully foster feelings of aggrieved superiority by segregating themselves from mankind, defying the mores of men, and permitting but one compatible spirit, a woman, to share in their insulated microuniverse. It seems doubtful that Byron meant them as exemplary persons or was unaware of what Jeffrey called their "morbid exaltation." Rather he illustrates that morbidity of will which is decisively analysed in *Parisina* by William H. Marshall (*The Structure*, pp. 62-71). The sublimity of characters such as Alp and Conrad, instead of embodying a state of transcendence, resembles a sort of defection from humanity, a perversely brave attachment to some crime, or an abnormally intense reaction to another's offense.

[9] *The Structure*, p. 136.

cast in the position of having to make some sort of direct choice between God and Lucifer, rather than Manfred-wise having an Abbot or a subaltern Spirit intruding upon his private universe.

But it becomes evident that Cain, if he grimly opposes God, also reduces Lucifer to an extension of himself, so that his real choice has to be made between the universe he knows and the universe he would desire, between the received conception of God and his preferred conception of himself. Lucifer, it is true, plays a conspicuous part in the first two of the play's three acts. He is the one who gives tongue most eloquently to the heroic spirit which undoubtedly moves in Cain: "Thou speak'st to me," the latter declares, "of things which long have swum / In visions through my thought." He is the one who whets Cain's heroicism by taking him on the voyage through the universe, leaving him the more "intoxicated with eternity," the more disgusted with his "dust." And all the time he pours into the ears of Cain his message subversive and inflaming, concerning

> Souls who dare use their immortality—
> Souls who dare look the Omnipotent tyrant in
> His everlasting face, and tell him that
> His evil is not good!

Yet it is doubtful that Lucifer can stand finally as a paramount figure in the drama, rivalling God in philosophy and Cain as a character. He is an evasive, rather than a seductive philosopher, at once incapable of moving Cain's mind into rhythm with his own and ill-prepared to counter the independent thrust of Cain's mind. He cannot cope with Cain's probing question about his happiness. Lucifer knows that his position is evil; Cain takes up a position that is basically conceived of as good. Thus Cain, though he looks akin to Lucifer, unequivocally "thirst[s] for good." The function of Lucifer is really to try to make Cain mean what he himself means when their statements coincide. He fares less than smoothly.

Nothing brings this out better than to compare him, as Byron did, with Milton's Satan (*LJ*, v, 469-470). Beside the temptation of Eve in *Paradise Lost*, where Satan draws his circle of enchantment segment by segment around the woman, the temptation of Cain appears monotonous and, worse, ineffectual. For Cain defies Lucifer: "I never / As yet have bow'd unto my father's god, / . . . Why should I bow to thee?"[10] In Byron's personal reading, "the object of the Demon is to *depress* [Cain] still further in his own estimation than he was before, by showing him infinite things and his own abasement, till he falls into the frame of mind that leads to the Catastrophe" (*LJ*, v, 470); but the play emphasizes aspiration rather than abasement, and renders Lucifer's guided tour otiose. As Bostetter recognizes, "Cain needs no trip with Lucifer to stir him up to the acts culminating in the death of Abel." Cain effectively sums up the trip as "inferior . . . to my desires / And my conceptions." Joseph praises Byron's portrayal of Lucifer on the grounds that the latter is made to provide "almost an echo of what is already in Cain's own mind" (*Byron, the Poet*, p. 117). In truth Lucifer amounts to less than an echo for the somewhat narcissistic Cain; in the end, no longer even the celestial tourist guide, he becomes al-

---

[10] Lucifer does claim Cain for his own, pointing out that "he who bows not to him has bow'd to me." But this is a matter of theological nicety, not a working truth in the drama.

most avuncular in advising Cain to resist tyranny and "form an inner world / In [his] own bosom," as a way of approaching "spiritual / Nature." And it would seem that the tempter should be considerably more. Byron was to make considerably more of him in *The Deformed Transformed*, where in the person of the Stranger we meet an enhanced Lucifer type, enterprising, attractively unfamiliar, speciously kind, strong, creative, and darkly, deeply sinister. Where Lucifer imperfectly reflects Cain's mind, the Stranger invents and establishes a new, and fatally selfish philosophy in Arnold's mind, and turns a case of domestic discontent into an occasion of pandemic cruelty and vice. In short, he cultivates the fallow Arnold according to his purpose and his way. But even here we start in a postlapsarian world, in which Arnold is rather bullied and fawning than blessedly meek. With a characteristic ellipsis Byron blanks out the supposedly historical perfect world and shows the certified world going from bad to worse.

Conforming to this bias, the universe of *Cain*, though finally slaughter and dismay break into it, is somehow drawn away from theology, temptation, and sin. The problems of the fallen archangel scarcely signify per se, in sharp contrast once again with the treatment of Satan in *Paradise Lost*. The problem of the play is first and last Cain's, the problem of a man who seeks to equate the logical ability to perceive imperfection with the practical ability to renounce and remove it. It is not a negligible problem, but the weight and depth of its presentation in *Cain* have, since Goethe, been as a rule sympathetically exaggerated. A more judicious view is taken by Jeffrey, who long ago remarked that Byron touched off the reader's susceptibility to doubt without bringing to the perennial debate either fresh insight or resolution; and it is worthwhile to recall the opinion of Oliver Elton that "Cain too often resembles an eighteenth-century heretic who rediscovers some elementary objections to the cruder forms of orthodoxy."[11]

Cain's quarrel with existence pivots around death and ironically carries him toward it. But he becomes the agent and producer of death, not just the occasion of a death, like Manfred. Thus, where Astarte's death is a catalytic or complicating factor in *Manfred*, Abel's death is veritably the crisis and climax of Cain's career. Through it he realizes the fallacy of his hopes and the real implications of his biases and deeds, the emptiness of his fiat and the disorder of his peculiar will. Without forgetting "the inadequacy of his state to his conceptions" (*LJ*, v, 270), he recognizes a new principle of conduct, the postlapsarian necessity of restraining passion and enduring pain. In the last analysis, the resignation and obedience of Adam appears indisputably courageous and good, though Byron honors Cain in his wilfulness. What is austere and practical provides an ambivalent measure for what is ecstatic in *Cain*, but overall the play goes much further than *Manfred* toward the championship of a catholic, though not an institutional orthodoxy. Perhaps nothing brings home to the reader the genuineness of Byron's, if not Cain's, conversion as graphically as the reversal of the typical time-sleep imagery of romanticism in Cain's stunned confession: "I am awake at last; a dreary dream / Had madden'd me"

---

[11] Jeffrey, "Lord Byron's Tragedies," *Edinburgh Review* (February 1822), pp. 288-289, and *A Survey*, p. 164, respectively. More recently Bernard Blackstone has suggested that in *Cain* Byron "is being wantonly provocative and, in consequence, rather tiresome" (*The Lost Travellers*, London, 1962, p. 183).

(Act III). Youth and the past here take on the quality of dismal and burdensome unreality which, even in Byron's own early poems, usually belongs to manhood and the present.

Significantly, though, *Cain* does not promise the realization of a new world. At play's end, as Adah wishes "Peace" to the spirit of the slain Abel, Cain illuminates his own tortured future with the cry: "But with me!—." The anxiety expressed by the Abbot in *Manfred* over the hero's future is here distilled into an expression of despair by the hero figure himself.

In Cain we may see graphically the two extreme and opposing capacities of the hero of self-will: to seduce the imagination, and to dismay the judgment. Both capacities come into play again as Byron turns from the fictional hero (Manfred) and the pseudo-fictional hero (Cain) to the historical and contemporary hero (Napoleon). Besides, with the latitude of the lyrical and narrative forms in the "Ode to Napoleon Buonaparte" and the pertinent stanzas of *Childe Harold*, Byron superadds personal evaluation and interpretation to the details of characterization, using a reflective and allusive technique to create a historical perspective and to forecast the judgment of time in a work on the surface preeminently topical, and instinct "with that quick spontaneity of his."[12] He thus places the portrayal of the hero against a background of political philosophy, indeed of political morality, to which the dramatic form seems less than hospitable in his hands.

The shock of Napoleon's fall being scarcely fresher in the poet's mind than the memory of his exaltation, the

[12] John Wain, "The Search for Identity," in *Byron: A Collection of Critical Essays*, ed. Paul West, New Jersey, 1963, p. 169.

"Ode" scours along the boundary between hero-worship and a throbbing, aggressive disillusionment, prompting Hazlitt to object that Byron was writing "both for [Napoleon] and against him." Its leitmotiv is the dichotomous idea of elevation and fall, rhetorically complemented by frequent use of oxymoron, paradox, and contrast. Its intricate nine-line stanza[13] too suggests both spontaneity and regulation, or an uncertainly regulated outburst. From its dogmatic opening phrase, " 'T is done," to the insistent superlatives of its final stanza the "Ode to Napoleon Buonaparte" is impassioned, even vehement work. The speaker, in the grip of intense feeling, hectically addresses now Napoleon, now the reader, now perhaps himself (see st. i, e.g.). The key to his volatility is to be found in the twelfth stanza:

> Weigh'd in the balance, hero dust
> Is vile as vulgar clay;[14]
> Thy scales, Mortality! are just
> To all that pass away:
> But yet methought the living great
> Some higher spark should animate,
> To dazzle and dismay:
> Nor deem'd Contempt could thus make mirth
> Of these, the Conquerors of the earth.

Let down by his "hero," he bitterly turns his habitual scorn of the vulgar and the vile on the erstwhile great man ("hero dust Is vile"). He presents this as a settled

[13] A4 B3 A4 B3 C4 C4 B3 D4 D4.
[14] Though he will continue to match Fielding in his aversion to the "great Man" of social and political reputation, Byron does not give over all distinctions between "clay" and "dust." In *Childe Harold* IV he sees in Dante, Petrarch, and Boccaccio an intrinsic and immortal excellence whereby their bones are "distinguish'd from our common clay / In death as life" (lvi).

verdict, not an angry charge; his opinion is "weigh'd" and, as his introduction of the concept of mortality attests, the hero is judged *sub specie aeternitatis*. But his judicial analysis masks the vindictiveness of a proud and thwarted worshipper. He, the speaker, has been "logically" (for that is the force of "should") credulous of "higher sparks" in his hero, and, having identified himself with him, implicitly suffers in his fall. Like Byron himself, he seems "utterly bewildered and confounded" (*LJ*, ii, 409). He is, however, spared the worst, since he has gained in knowledge. The hero now serves as a "lesson" (st. iii), and repels the judgment that had been in abeyance while yet he was able to overpower the imagination, to "dazzle" instead of "dismay."

The terms of the "lesson" make the "Ode" a virtual counterweight to *Manfred*, stressing blame and largely leaving praise to be inferred, while that play insinuates blame and stresses praise. The speaker is free with "contempt," if not with "mirth"—he is too involved for that. He twice calls Napoleon a "thing" (i, ix); he dubs him "Dark Spirit" and "All Evil Spirit" (iv, ix), after directly comparing him to Satan in the first stanza (ll.8-9). These different forms of condemnation complement rather than contradict each other. Napoleon, stripped of his "purple vest," proves subject to all he had seemed born to subject others to: "The Desolator desolate! / The Victor overthrown! / The Arbiter of others' fate / A Suppliant for his own." He proves no better than a "thing" of "vulgar clay." That is his nature, his being. The consequences of his being are another matter, though: Napoleon has strewn "our earth with hostile bones," has emulated "scourge" and "earthquake," acting as a "vain forward child of Empire," with men and nations alike for his "playthings." In short, he is diabolical in his fruits, in himself "little worth." But the fact remains that he has been "long obey'd," has been "a King" for whom "Earth has spilt her blood." The problem of change, offspring of time and extension of mortality, comes to a head here, and is aggravated by the recognition that Napoleon has brought heroism to a new nadir in failing to die "as honour dies" (st. xi).

In its final four stanzas (xvi-xix) the "Ode" pivots toward a possible resolution of this crux. Where before Byron has invoked historical figures such as Charles V or Dionysus II for purposes of comparison in the temporal order, he now brings up mythological and biblical figures, Prometheus and Satan, as speculative models out of an absolute framework. The crisis of opinion gives rise to reflection on what the hero might be. For the speaker, if rationally "cured" of hero-worship, remains psychologically predisposed toward it; in his own person, of course, Byron wrote: "I won't give [Napoleon] up even now" (*LJ*, ii, 410). In Prometheus and Satan are seen sublime superiority to adversity and pain, superiority to the effects and thus to the existence of change; this is what Prometheus and Satan have in common, and what constitutes the ideal might-have-been for Napoleon. He should have shown Promethean or Satanic fortitude in his downfall, instead of "hoarding" his blood (st. x). More than this, he should have risen above even his better fortune, and have "resigned" his "immeasurable power." The poem here seems to veer away from a concern with practical affairs to a primarily conceptual attitude, appearing nearly akin to *Manfred* in its equal indifference to power and pain. The introduction of Washington's name in the last stanza, though it returns us to a historical and practical bearing, still keeps philosophical postulates in mind. The individual action, or perhaps rather the question of personal choice, is under assessment not just in terms of what gives rise to it (personality), but also in terms of what it results in (history).

To this point the hero "of thousand thrones"—the phrase may recall Helen of Troy and the launching of a thousand ships—has been exposed as a man of inner paltriness, at the mercy of change; his place has been taken by the Promethean hero, who knows but defies change; and the Promethean hero has in turn given way to the self-denying hero, who creates change for the good of others without getting entangled in the process of change, and who proves himself indifferent to material state. This is Washington, who stands as the reverse of Napoleon: a man who is great and at the same time greatly good, outstanding in the liberal use of his power, mighty in service. In him many strands of the "Ode to Napoleon Buonaparte" are neatly tied together: the concept of the hero is salvaged, the bleak pattern of history relieved, and the perils of time and change avoided, insofar as there has been found a hero who is a hero for good, one who *has* used his "power to save" *to save*, and who has even curbed the malice of human nature ("envy dared not hate" him). Still the conclusion of the "Ode" is not wholly affirmative. Washington stands as the first and last of his kind. How immediate, then, and how relevant a standard can the version of heroism he embodies provide? How nearly can he touch the imagination that moves and commits to action, as opposed to the imagination that waits and yearns? Can he begin to take the imaginative center of the poem away from Napoleon, or does he only take a place as a singular phenomenon in a Napoleonic cosmos? It would appear, in truth, that Washington comes into the poem under the spontaneous pressure of the question which introduces the last stanza: "Where may the wearied eye repose. . . ?" He has been rather snatched than built into the "Ode," apparently as a desperate gesture on the part of a speaker who cannot quite cope with the contradictions of human personality or the confusions of human history epitomized by Napoleon's case.

In *Childe Harold* iii a few years later, Byron was to use Marceau instead of Washington to exemplify "Freedom's champion,"[15] but he was to seem even less positive than on 10 April 1814 about the characteristics and stature of Napoleon (his view of the Corsican Alexander remains unsettled up to "The Age of Bronze"). Forthrightly speaking in his own person Byron displays the same spread-eagled duality of feeling that made him, in "Napoleon's Farewell," call the hero's page in French history "brightest or blackest." Nearly a dozen expressions of ambivalence or indecision crowd into the six stanzas (xxxvi-xli) devoted to Napoleon proper, with the dubious justification that Napoleon's spirit—and not the writer's—is "antithetically mixt"; as Hazlitt irritably reflected, "Buonaparte's character, be it what else it may, does not change every hour according to his Lordship's varying humour. . . . Why should Lord Byron now laud him to the skies in the hour of his success, and then peevishly wreak his disappointment on the God of his idolatry?" But of course Byron is measuring "character" against public reputation, fact against opinion, analysis against emotion. And the result is not clear. It is pos-

---

[15] For obvious reasons the number of those who wield freedom's weapons has increased to a "few."

sible to dismiss Napoleon, and all "the madmen who have made men mad" (xlii, xlv). But that will decide nothing as long as it is necessary to admit that his "wild name / Was ne'er more bruited in men's minds than now" (xxxvii), necessary to admit his "contagion," and impossible to resolve whether he is "god" or "nothing." Napoleon's status as hero and Byron's as worshipper-turned-analyst imply a perpetual motion of self-renouncing extremes.

It appears erroneous to take *Childe Harold* III to be "a sympathetic investigation of madness."[16] The stanzas on Napoleon chime with the rest in their turbulent alternations and revisions of viewpoint, virtually amounting to a portrait of ambivalence, a portrait of the analytical mind's failure to extinguish an unwarranted commitment.

Clearly while Byron was very jealous of the human "right of thought," which he termed "our last and only place / Of refuge," thought or "reason" meant for him a chance to stave off subjugation and despair rather than a way to salvation (*CH* IV.cxxvii). Beside Wordsworth's "last place of refuge—my own soul," Byron's "right of thought" suggests an abstract capacity, not an ontological *sine qua non*; it is impersonally conceived, "our" instead of "my" place of refuge, and moreover it is universally, in the nature of things, "chain'd and tortured." Byron undoubtedly had a sharp, spontaneous bent toward the indomitable mind or will with which as a rule critics associate his name. But time and again that bent is checked by the poet's reflective, qualifying habit of mind. One

[16] W. J. Calvert, *Byron: Romantic Paradox*, Chapel Hill, North Carolina, 1935, p. 146, with a concurring judgment by M. K. Joseph, *Byron the Poet*, p. 96.

may suggest that after all what stands as Byronic is the perennial psychomachia of the indomitable mind-as-will and an indefatigable analysis.[17]

Byron in fact writes an implicit palinode to the immortal "beings of the mind" in *Childe Harold* IV, and as a substitute entertains the idea of "strong reality" (sts. v-vi). But *Manfred* and *Cain* and the "Ode to Napoleon Buonaparte" and *Childe Harold* III foretell nothing but difficulty in encountering reality in a world with "all things weigh'd in custom's falsest scale" and "Opinion an omnipotence

whose veil

Mantles the earth with darkness, until right
And wrong are accidents, and men grow pale
Lest their own judgments should become too bright,
And their free thoughts be crimes,
and earth have too much light."

    (*CH* IV.xciii)

A certain ungainly indecisiveness marks Byron's position on the will as a reflection of the clash between his faith in the autonomous mind and his knowledge of reality. The Corsair Conrad's authority is said to reflect

---

[17] The conventional meaning of "Byronic," as of "Machiavellian," took root so rapidly and has been nurtured so long as to have grown into an indispensable cultural landmark. What Leslie A. Marchand sums up as a "haughty romantic melancholy of a defiant and Satanic turn" (*Selected Poetry*, intro., p. v) may forever be designated Byronic; certainly that designation has persisted from Jeffrey and Goethe to Bertrand Russell and modern literary criticism. It is, nevertheless, an unhappily misleading form of critical synecdoche, which has conceded very little to the recognition in Byron's work of "a tough-minded realism and a trenchant satire . . . always grounded in a basic sanity and a knowledge of human nature" (*ibid.*). Still, our conception of Byronic melancholy and indomitability may be susceptible, from within, of a critical as opposed to a cultural qualification.

"The power of Thought—the magic of the Mind! ("The Corsair," I, viii); but don't his career and his vaguely desolate end, to say nothing of Medora's, betray the liability of the mind to the harsh play of circumstances? "The Sonnet on Chillon" celebrates the "Eternal Spirit of the chainless Mind" as a prelude to "The Prisoner of Chillon." Then "The Prisoner" presents a mind that had been "Proud of persecution's rage" increasingly dispirited by a standard course of physical and spiritual deprivation, and ultimately brought "to love despair" (1. 374) and to look on prison as "a second home" (1. 380).[18] The primary power of circumstances is confessed in what I take as the moral of the Tale: "a long communion tends / To make us what we are" (ll. 390-391). The poem, moreover, though this moral appears neutral, virtually insists that it be pessimistically construed.[19] When Bonnivard gets to look out on the world of nature from his "barr'd window," after who knows how many years, how many "summers with the length / Of . . . long winters," he merely becomes "troubled" and wishes he had not left his "recent chain." He is oppressed, not restored by beauty and grace he has seen, and it is clear as he lowers himself back to the floor of his jail that he will never be restored:

[18] The inconsistency between the "Sonnet" and "The Prisoner" is cogently argued by Marshall in *The Structure*, pp. 82-96.

[19] At the cost of a grave historical distortion, as Byron soon learned. His statement, in a note to the poem, that he would "have endeavoured to dignify the subject by an attempt to celebrate [Bonnivard's] courage and . . . virtues" if he had known enough about him at the time of writing need not pass unchallenged. The fact that he found inspiration in the Bonnivard of imagination is substantive. Nothing in the poem suggests that it was written "to order," as a sort of laureate piece. Speculation on the poem Byron presumably would have produced on the Bonnivard of history would seem idle enough.

The darkness of my dim abode
Fell on me as a heavy load;
It was as in a new-dug grave
Closing o'er one we sought to save.

Spent perhaps from the very effort of climbing, of aspiration, he is laid in ultimate misery. The imagery of death expresses more than a state of subjective despair; it is the realization in the individual mind of the presence of death in nature, a presence already betrayed where the singing bird (a nightingale? a skylark?) so poignantly tempted identification with the "eternal spirit," and then itself proved "mortal" (l. 290). Time, and change, in effect, can undo but cannot recreate a man. And they will undo an anti-social figure such as Conrad (who however desires not license but good), and also the patriotic Bonnivard. Thus where Wordsworth's little girl can say "we are seven" with philosophical as well as dramatic validity, Byron's old man—the contrast in age epitomizes the opposition of views—must mourn that "we *were* seven" ("The Prisoner of Chillon," l. 17, italics added). One might imagine Bonnivard as a Washington, or at least as a Prometheus; this potential hero, in accordance with what seems an intrinsic quality in the universe and his mind, has been annihilated as a hero, and as a soul with any sort of romantically supereminent faculty of will. The poem by anticipation gives the lie to Byron's assumption, in *The Age of Bronze*, that a hero "plunged in a dungeon" still can be "great."

The portraits of Byron's heroes initially display an unharmonized range of confrontations between the autonomous mind-as-will and "strong reality." Nor does the principle of reconciliation and order come readily to hand; the outstanding common element in the portraits may be taken to be the evocation of a state of antinomy. In having his fictive persons question whether Manfred is sanctified or damned, whether Napoleon is "more or less than man," Byron gives voice to a moral and epistemological quandary in a world where the hero of all-overleaping will is glorified for his will while yet the Aristotelian test of use and measure holds good and discloses a guilty excess of will. Again, it is odd that Cain's will, breeding murder in its egocentric vehemence, when corrected proves barren of fruit; the enlightened Cain has no viable future. Even where the will is intrinsically virtuous and staunch, a new paradox is all that emerges: Washington and Marceau produce novelty, not change, something that is great but ephemeral; and it can be noted in passing that Sardanapalus, who offers an engaging if not a typically virtuous vision, seeks in vain to implement it in a needful but unyielding world. Finally, in the case of Bonnivard, a presumably virtuous and staunch will is undone by the indifferent and irresistible process of time. If, as Byron seems to say, something in the nature of experience puts a premium on individual will, one is also tempted to observe the fundamental antinomy that something in the nature of things is inhospitable to it.

The protean subject of the hero provides a nearly exhaustive context[20] for the early culture of a conception of "strong reality." Not that Byron conducts a scientific experiment. *Manfred* and *Cain* are passionate adventures in the field of reality, the "Ode to Napoleon

[20] The impasse in Byron's position on the will is broken where he develops the viability of the stoical mean, of the will to endure. See above, fn. 8, and Chap. V below.

Buonaparte" and *Childe Harold* III passionate analyses of it. Here the all but pedantic positiveness of such works as *English Bards* and *Childe Harold* I and II dissolves into a pattern of questioning. If we follow Byron further into the world of "reality" or fact, into *Childe Harold* IV and the rich earthy triad of comic narratives, we find the problem of certitude or of truth more overt, more urgent. Though he made the problem an occasion of wry or ribald jesting, Byron was not one who "would not wait for an answer." Rather he pursued one in ways and with results unusual in his time. All the younger romantic poets had their quarrel with language for failing them in the expression of ultimate experience: "What we have of feeling most intense / Outstrips our faint expression" (*CH* IV.clviii); but Byron alone persistently quarrelled with the effect of language in everyday usage. He perceived an ever-present threat of tendentiousness and of inert mechanism in the business of naming actions and beliefs, realizing how eagerly opinion and conduct, owing to what Wittgenstein has called "the bewitchment of our intellect by means of language," moved to the tune of words that they should call. Ultimately he recognized the great power that is "in a name," and so he challenged the words he was, as a human being and poet, unable to go without. Byron appears close to anticipating the orientation of modern linguistic philosophy in his poetry as, without sustaining the verbal richness of a Keats or the noble conviction of a Wordsworth, it develops the sinewy beauty of an intellect seeking intimacy with passion, of intense feeling seeking the foundation of reason.

BYRON AND THE
WORLD OF FACT

*The world is a perpetual caricature of itself;
at every moment it is the mockery and the
contradiction of what it is pretending to be.*
GEORGE SANTAYANA

Hours of Idleness, Byron's early portmanteau of assorted
experimental poems, offers in the lines "To Romance" a
remarkable preview of his teetering between irreconcilable positions which can be characterized as idealism
and actuality, knowledge (or perhaps intellect acting
upon empirical knowledge) and faith. Byron renounces
romance, but he does so with ill-concealed regret: " 't is
hard to quit the dreams / Which haunt the unsuspicious
soul." Similarly, his equating of romance with "childish
joys" loses some of its authority when we see that his new
attitude grows out of disillusionment, not maturity. Even
as he offers his strictures on romance, which is now "but
a name," a purely fabricated world of "deceit" and "Af-
fectation" and "sickly Sensibility," he is forced to be correspondingly hard on himself as erstwhile believer
("Fond fool"). Evidently he as well as his world must
be changed.

The terms of the change, however, seem neither consistent nor feasible. Does Byron "leave [the] realm"
of romance (st. 1) or do they "perish" in "oblivion's
blackening lake" (st. 8)? In other words, does he create
or only passively witness change? To compound the
problem, the poem is rather imprecise in representing

the "Truth" supposed to take the place of the "realms of air." It is so overwhelmingly given over to describing and decrying romance that the protestation, "[I] leave thy realms for those of Truth," suggests a fairly vague inclination toward an object, rather than an assured destination. If the past world is certainly dead for the poet, the new one—truth not being a product of mere volition —seems almost as certainly powerless to be born.[1]

The clue to this failure on both fronts lies in the fact that Byron is unwittingly "flying" from discovered Truth no less than from exposed Romance. One presupposes the other, and differs from it only in direction of focus. But Byron, ready for neither literary realism nor practical cynicism, somehow keeps at arm's length the poem's only tangible truth, that romantic courtesy is a hypochondriacal hypocrisy. It is all too clear that he is "leaving," or rather yearning "for [realms] of Truth" which genuinely will embody spirituality, friendship, and fidelity; he is in a special way raising the desirable over the actual, the ideal over the known. Though formality of tone and of diction, and a tight structural regularity give the poem the air of an embryonic ode to rationality, Byron perhaps betrays its latent bias by entitling it "To Romance."

Elsewhere in *Hours of Idleness* he designates his muse as "the simple truth" ("Answer to Some Elegant Verses"). But this can amount to no more than an argumentative challenge offered at once to contemporary literature and to himself. A reliable mark of his resolved position presents itself in the complications and mutations of his

---

[1] Ridenour reads the poem essentially as a "Popean" opposition of truth to romance (*Style*, pp. 92-93); this is somewhat oversimplified, and entails an unfortunate distortion of the temper of Byron's work.

"truth."[2] Beyond the evidence already brought up, we find Byron in effect defying his muse: "Truth!—wherefore did thy hated beam / Awake me to a world like this?" ("I Would I Were a Careless Child"). In this cry he makes explicit the aversion to crude material truth which gives rise to subconscious tension in "To Romance." A higher and more comprehensive truth appears momentarily as the object of Childe Harold's aspirations (II.xxvii.6-9), but disappointment here proves correspondingly keener and more definitive, as the hero cannot even become acquainted with that truth—it is as inaccessible as swarming facts are insistent. And Byron conveys the impression that an innate incapacity causes the Childe's frustration, for "as he gazed on truth his aching eyes grew dim" (l. 9). Whether the eyes ache from straining to see or from inability to accommodate the sight, the result is the bleak negation implied in the phrase "grew dim."

On that sort of negation, as a matter of fact, Byron has no monopoly in the romantic period. We may recall John Wilson's troubled acknowledgement of the "subjects of darkness and mystery which afford, at some period or other in his life, so much disquiet . . . so much agony to the mind of every reflecting modern."[3] And it is clear that a certain negation takes a central place in the "Ode to a Nightingale," in the "Ode: Intimations of Immortal-

---

[2] Ruskin in *Praeterita* praises Byron for his "measured and living *truth*" (*Works*, ed. Cook and Wadderburn, xxxv, 148), but this can only be truth as a summary abstraction and distillation from the Byron corpus, the perception that made Ruskin call Byron "the truest . . . Seer of the Nineteenth Century" (xxxiv, 397). It is not any of the truths which attracted and exercised Byron.

[3] "Childe Harold's Pilgrimage: Canto the Fourth," *Edinburgh Review*, xxx (1818), 96.

ity," and in "Dejection: An Ode," besides being at least thematically important in such poems as the "Hymn to Intellectual Beauty" and "Europe: A Prophecy." A potentially disabling apprehension of mortality and finitude is not easily separated from the imaginative transcendency of romanticism. Byron claims special attention, in the last analysis, in that he tries such a miscellany of nostrums against mortality: the inexhaustible will, for example, tradition (artistic *or* historical), nature as direct metaphysical healer *or* as propitious symbol, the mystical spirit of youth, personal love, "the right of thought" . . . ; and in that he so candidly details its protean recrudescence.

His aggravated difficulty in reaching a state of belief may be advantageously compared with Blake's vigorously masculine assumption of the apocalyptic world. Blake charges the individual or the age, rather than the intrinsic condition of the universe, with any failure of faith.

> Then I asked: does a firm perswasion that a thing
> is so, make it so? He replied. All poets believe that it
> does, & in ages of imagination this firm perswasion
> removed mountains; but many are not capable of a
> firm perswasion of any thing.
>
> *The Marriage of Heaven and Hell*

> VI. If any could desire what he is incapable of possessing, despair must be his eternal lot.
> VII. The desire of Man being Infinite, the possession is Infinite & himself Infinite.
>
> "There Is No Natural Religion" [6][4]

[4] Cited from *The Poetry and Prose of William Blake*, ed. David V. Erdman with commentary by Harold Bloom, New York, 1965.

A settled serenity, a settled vigor revealed in the language and rhythm of these excerpts will almost surely dispose the reader toward sharing in Blake's conviction; so will a somewhat less self-evident feature of the lines, an implicitly argumentative rhetoric. With phrase upon phrase, "but many are not capable," "if . . . , [then] . . . must be," "[this] being [the case] . . . , [it therefore follows] . . . ," Blake erects an unobtrusive wall of logic to impede opposition and to buttress his own propositions.

In Byron's work this sidelong, perhaps even subliminal recognition of adverse possibilities swings into the center of attention, largely we may suppose, because he expected an "age of imagination" to cope with a disorderly "repertory of facts" (*DJ* xiv.xiii), and because he saw no escape from "the inadequacy of [our] state to [our] conceptions."[5] According to Blake, the desire of man being infinite, the possession is infinite. With his less categorical habits of mind, Byron could not have so serenely abolished the other possibility in logic, that his destitution might be so. This is not to suggest that Byron's position looks desperate or defeatist. He is kept from that in the first place by the very inconclusiveness of the analytical process, and even more important by his own unquenchable desire[6] for the sort of dream ("To

[5] Byron was not alone in seeing a need to be on guard against prejudice that passes under a cloak of philosophy. Coleridge, for one, may have known the dangers even more thoroughly than he. But Coleridge, as Judson S. Lyon points out, "for all his critical alertness [to the dangers and limitations of inner-sense figures], found such figures so apt to some of his psychological endeavors and so common in the works of the thinkers who most influenced him, that he often ignored his own caveats, and used them freely" ("Romantic Psychology and the Inner Senses: Coleridge," *PMLA*, LXXXI [1966], 249).

[6] See E. D. Hirsch, Jr., "Byron and the Terrestrial Paradise," in *From Sensibility to Romanticism*, pp. 467-486.

Edward Noel Long, Esq.") or truth (*Childe Harold*) which is self-sufficient, stable, beautiful, and withal potent against the confusions of the empirical order. Surely an almost puritanical desire plays a large part in his refusal of seductive substitutes for truth.

His concern for facts nevertheless engenders a problem of evaluation. Keats cried Byron down for representing what he had seen, rather than what he imagined (he himself found the matter of imagination to be like Adam's dream, not like the Redcrosse Knight's); but Ruskin praised Byron on those very grounds, saying that he "spoke only of what he had seen, and known; and spoke without exaggeration, without mystery, without enmity, and without mercy" (*Works*, xxxv, 149). The issue between Keats and Ruskin, it will be found, is essentially superficial; the expression of praise or blame tends to obscure the way both writers conceive of Byron's work as strong in receptivity, not in creativity, as attaining to reproductive credibility but wanting in imaginative or conceptual authority. Indeed Byron vaunted himself on his fidelity to fact. Though we need not be credulous of his claims—*Sardanapalus* has only the most exiguous foundation in history, and the liberties Byron takes with his source material for *Marino Faliero* indicate a very elastic obedience to facts—the proposition that he is a poet of the seen gets undeniable support from the want of an imposing, or imposed philosophical unity in his work, and even more from the material use of himself as a subject. Yet there is a compatibility, even a sort of continuity among the elements, insofar as they make up a spectrum of obligatory responses to an experimental, or at best obscurely regulated, order. The apparent self-display of Byron's work may have the stamp and the value of a positively human independence-cum-humility: he deals with himself, like Thoreau perhaps, as the subject on which he is best qualified to speak, making himself a legitimate point of departure for more inclusive discussion. It is important to note, moreover, that he deals with himself, and with his "facts," in terms having the insistence of experience or evidence, rather than of dogma. The fluid character of his work may likewise convey not a wanton stirring up but a precise vision of the encountered world.

Byron's lifelong habit of making self-conscious—if not self-explanatory—references to his style gives prima facie support to the contention that his most "licentious" work has not a random form, but an unconventional, rationally chosen form, and would also tend to reveal the mere proposition that he sees, his "repertory of facts," as no more than a prelude to recognition of the way he sees, of the conceptual implications of subject matter and form. One is wary of dictating a convenient pattern into the copiousness and variety of, say, *Don Juan*; but it is to be remembered that Byron's handling of his material, though often emotionally descriptive or dramatic in immediacy and involvement, as a rule takes direction from a reflective, even abstractive frame of mind.

On the strength of the remarks Byron made in situations free from polemics, it is easy to conclude that the "cosmos" of his poetry is "*feeling* not intellect" (Clement Tyson Goode, *Byron as Critic*, Weimar, 1923, p. 86). Byron associates poetry with compelling, unWordsworthian emotion and inarticulate, obscure visions of "new" man.

What is Poesy but to create
From overfeeling Good and Ill; and aim
At an external life beyond our fate,
And be the new Prometheus of new men. . . ?
"The Prophecy of Dante," IV, 11-14

What is Poetry?—the feeling of a Former world
and a Future.
(*LJ*, v, 189)
Are not the *passions* the food and fuel of poesy?
(*LJ*, v, 55)
Poetry is the expression of an *excited passion*.
(*LJ*, v, 318)

And the emotion identified with poetry has about it
something pathological: the impulse to poetry reveals,
the production of poetry relieves a virulence in the
creator.

Poetry is the lava of the imagination whose
eruption prevents an earthquake.
(*LJ*, III, 405; see also *Childe Harold* III.iv)

And the unquiet feelings which first woke
Song in the world, will seek what then they sought;
As on the beach the waves at last are broke,
Thus to the extreme verge the passions brought
Dash into poetry, which is but passion. . . .
(*Don Juan* IV.cvi)

As poetry for Byron precludes self-possession, it readily
turns into a sort of possession:

As for poesy, mine is the *dream* of my sleeping
Passions; when they are awake, I cannot speak
their language, only in their Somnambulism.
(*LJ*, IV, 43)

The emphasis on incontinent passion in all the foregoing statements culminates in a dictum which could as well be an indictment of much of Augustan poetry, and in particular of the *Essay on Man*:

> Poetry is in itself passion, and does not system-
> atize. It assails, but does not argue; it may be
> wrong, but it does not assume pretensions to
> Optimism.
>   (*LJ*, v, 582)

Still the passion Byron claims for poetry is not uncensored, not unalloyed by measures of knowledge and logic. Perhaps it would be most accurate to say that passion, in Byron's case, governs the inception of poetry more completely than its process or content. He shows reflection and passion combined, though not reconciled.

We might note that despite the common assumption that Byron is characteristically given to "admiration of heroic activity" (Joseph, p. 126), remarkably few of his heroes rank among men of prowess. They are heroes who bear the primary stamp of consciousness—of elected indomitability, of careful aloofness and gloom, of contemptuous intelligence and passion. They are little given to action; at one extreme they even, like Don Juan, largely give up practical choice. But they all either exercise the "right of thought" to a critical degree (e.g., Sardanapalus or Mazeppa), or they are met in a context critically colored by its exercise (e.g., Don Juan or Napoleon).

It will hardly seem surprising then that the question of knowledge should occupy a central position in Byron's work. The protean elusiveness of certitude—facts being relentless but not necessarily clear—furnishes a highlight for his adopted ottava rima stanza equally with his most sustained philosophical disquisition. He may set himself up as the celebrant of the world of fact, but he is also partly its victim, one who comes into it with an initial bias toward hope and love, and as a seeker after truth. It is as such that he develops the negative reflex of characterizing it as a wilderness of fact, and more aggressively, of maintaining with volleys of logic and laughter the unbalancing relation of seeker and universe. To study the apparent confusions of imagery and structure in his work, and the apparent rootlessness of his attitudes toward characters, actions, and ideas is to see them as strategies, as means to a comprehensive end which, paradoxically perhaps, exchanges the hieratic finality of "I affirm" for the profane unpredictability of "I would affirm." Hence what one may call the imagery of contradiction in *Don Juan*, "Mazeppa," and *Childe Harold* iii-iv.[7]

With the ambivalent proposal, already seen, that Napoleon's page in French history is the "brightest or blackest," Byron graphically indicates how the tortuous ways of experience baffle and betray the aim of judgment. Of course, each of the alternatives may be preferred to the other, but neither can be denied; each conclusion is valid without invalidating its antithesis. This kind of rhetorical impasse occurs often enough to be of moment in Byron's work, and is unusual enough to war-

[7] For other discussions of Byron's imagery, with different emphases from mine, see Ernest J. Lovell, Jr., "Irony and Image in *Don Juan*," in *English Romantic Poets: Modern Essays in Criticism*, ed. M. H. Abrams, New York, 1960, pp. 228ff.; M. K. Joseph, *Byron the Poet*, London, 1964, pp. 212ff.; and John William Harrison, "The Imagery of Byron's Romantic Narratives and Dramas," Univ. of Colorado Ph.D., 1958, L.C. Card no. Mic 59-829.

rant special attention. Byron clearly poses a problem different from what we meet in the *Epistle to Dr. Arbuthnot* where Pope writes: "All Bedlam or Parnassus is let out." No real choice is invited, or possible, between Bedlam and Parnassus. The "Bedlamites" have ludicrously usurped the name of Parnassus, but since they must remain what they are, their "Parnassus" equals Bedlam—the two terms become convertible, one: as Boileau would have it: "C'est en vain qu'au Parnasse le téméraire auteur / Pense de l'art des vers atteindre la hauteur." Far from thus signalizing sameness by the appearance of opposition, Byron offers a real but indissoluble opposition, where no one seems to know more or better than his adversary, where not just a particular standard of judgment, but the very operation of judgment is called into question.

We meet a different problem, again, in Spenser's ascribing the turmoil of the Redcrosse Knight to "unwonted lust, or wonted fear of doing aught amiss." Though evidently in conflict, and on the surface holding out minimum grounds for choice, this fear and lust somehow also reinforce each other and enjoy a mutual symmetry—the degree of fear reflects the intensity of the temptation. The symmetry is, however, highly precarious; the alternative, lust *or* fear, may well be regarded as an alternation of emotion, an indication of rapid but limited turbulence. With Spenser, opposition is immediately qualified and is peculiar to the passing occasion, rather than, as with Byron, occurring in the nature of things.

Pope's approach, and Spenser's, holding up in principle at least a general standard of judgment, prevails in poetry right through the romantic period.[8] It is almost to be expected, then, that the new tack Byron takes maintains itself on more than an ambivalent particle.[9] Ambivalence, or readiness to face up to duality—Byron might call it reality—occurs in a variety of forms in his work, and perhaps nowhere more notably than in his use of imagery and allusion. One finds images that are applied to a single person or situation seemingly at odds with one another; the same image applied to dissimilar persons or situations; and allusions to a single source so manipulated as to throw credit and blame on one character or situation, or else either credit or blame on

[8] The poet who most strikingly anticipates Byron, so far as I have found, is Andrew Marvell, in "The Character of Holland" and preeminently in "An Horatian Ode," with its pervasive and unfaltering dualism. In fact Byron's treatment of Cromwell (*CH* iv.lxxxv) has much in common with Marvell's. Among modern poets Yeats makes continual use of the imagery of contradiction: major images—the song, the dream, the bird—are put to paradoxical use in poems ranging from the "Song of the Happy Shepherd" to "Sailing to Byzantium"; Eliot also uses it, in a somewhat manneristic way.

[9] Other examples may be given a quick survey. In Fez, "all is Eden, or a wilderness" (*DJ* iv.liv); hell-fire is said to be prepared for people who give "Pleasure or pain to one another" (*DJ* ii.cxcii); Gulbeyaz has the beauty to make "A Kingdom or confusion anywhere" (*DJ* v.cxxix); Byron declares in *Childe Harold* that "Man with his God must strive: / Or, it may be, with demons" (iv.xxxiv), and again he interprets Napoleon's response to "the turning tide" as "wisdom, coldness, or deep pride" (iii.xxxix). The stanzas following the description of the Fez and those leading up to the comment on Napoleon also abound in oscillations of viewpoint which, though not always dependent on the ambiguous "or," help to show how intimately it is bound up with Byron's way of seeing. One final example will all but explicitly sum up the operation of the particle: "Juan [was] flatter'd by her [Catherine's] love, or lust;— / I cannot stop to alter words once written, / And the two are so mix'd up with human dust, / That he who *names one*, both perchance may hit on" (*DJ* ix.lxxvii); and Byron repeats the indistinguishable alternative, "love or lust," in xii.iv.

antagonistic characters or situations.[10] The effect is the gradual establishment of an almost schematic displacement that can offer an unusual, if not a comfortable perspective on the familiar world.

A combination of images occurring in two separate stanzas of *Childe Harold* illustrates the indifference Byron may be said to show to our habitual experience and expectation. The first stanza, from Canto III, deprecates man's aspirations by means of the images of mountain-top and tempest.

> He who ascends to mountain-tops, shall find
> The loftiest peaks most wrapt in clouds and snow;
> He who surpasses or subdues mankind,
> Must look down on the hate of those below.
> Though high *above* the sun of glory glow,
> And far *beneath* the earth and ocean spread,
> *Round* him are icy rocks, and loudly blow
> Contending tempests on his naked head,
> And thus reward the toils which to
> those summits led.
>
> (xlv)

The second stanza, from Canto IV, celebrates man's triumph over adversity in terms of the same images:

[10] The phenomenon described here may recall the romantic "contraries," which Blake and Coleridge and Wordsworth severally recognize and exploit. But Byron is not aiming at that dialectical synthesis or reconciliation of "opposite and discordant qualities" which was, according to Charles J. Smith, "almost a compulsion" for Wordsworth ("The Contrarieties: Wordsworth's Dualistic Imagery," *PMLA*, LXIX [1954], 1193). This in part because he is more interested than Wordsworth in the distinctive logic of events, and in part because, if he "strains" after a "cosmic philosophy" and a "monistic faith" (G. Wilson Knight, *The Burning Oracle*, Oxford, 1939, p. 280), he does so by probing experience for unforeseen possibilities of analysis of its Gordian knot, not by striking it through.

But from their nature will the tannen grow
Loftiest on loftiest and least sheltered rocks,
Rooted in barrenness, where nought below
Of soil supports them 'gainst the Alpine shocks
Of eddying storms; yet springs the trunk, and mocks
The howling tempest, till its height and frame
Are worthy of the mountains from whose blocks
Of bleak, gray granite into life it came,
And grew a giant tree;—the mind may
        grow the same.
 (xx)

This self-contrasted imagery met within one poem and one year is articulated with key parallels that rule out the possibility of haphazard composition; both passages weight the meaning of mountain and tempest by bringing in a variable relation of what is above to what is below, and by rating man according to the security of his purchase in his environment. The absence of actual effort to go higher, and indeed the absence of a higher point to go toward in the second excerpt can be acknowledged as material without qualification of the basic point that Byron has skillfully reused and reformed a single complex of terms. The reformation is easy enough to analyze, if not to assimilate. In iii.xlv Byron summarizes the state of things as done and known (shall, must); in iv.xx he enunciates a possibility, an appealing prospect (may). How, though, are the two related? How, and where, will the world of fact and the world of promise meet? The uncanny repetition of the images of one world in the other poses a problem virtually epistemological, and that problem cannot well be attempted until we see how Byron exploits the protean versatility of his images not simply at the point of presentation but also in reminiscent or associated passages.

The two passages in question prima facie bespeak man's vain ambition, and contrariwise his inborn power; but associated stanzas in both cantos quietly upset such impressions and further complicate the process of definition. The man who appears in a dramatic moment of failure in III.xlv is not ultimately derided; something like a compassionate regard for him supervenes by virtue of the forty-seventh stanza, where the man who aspires survives, indeed withstands the failure of his aspiration:

> And there they [castles] stand,
> > as stands a lofty mind,
> Worn, but unstooping to the baser crowd,
> All tenantless, save to the crannying wind,
> Or holding dark communion with the cloud.

For in these lines "unstooping to the baser crowd" and "holding dark communion with the cloud" make positive, in terms of spiritual character and quality, two adverse outward circumstances of the earlier stanza: peaks capped with clouds and the hate of the earthbound. We have in effect gone past accidents and variables which exalt or degrade a man (xlv) and come to a bare but far from inconsiderable minimum (xlvii).

A comparable revision is in evidence between IV.xx and IV.xxi. The active, irresistible self-achievement of the mind shifts toward a passive state of elementary stoicism, in which one does not wonderfully "spring" and "grow" but "bear."

> Existence may be borne, and the deep root
> Of life and sufferance make its firm abode
> In bare and desolated bosoms: mute

The camel labours with the heaviest load,
And the wolf dies in silence,—not bestow'd
In vain should such example be; if they,
Things of ignoble or of savage mood,
Endure and shrink not, we of nobler clay
May temper it to bear,—it is but for a day.

This compounded qualification of point of view, with images revising themselves and continually undergoing further adjustment in context, is a legitimate procedure for any writer and, for Byron, works basically as a refinement of a total picture, or perhaps rather an adventure in inclusiveness. The first two cantos reveal Byron explicitly concerned with the confusions of experience— the words "mingle," "mix," and "blend," as often as not appear without overtones of harmony, solution, or integration. Again and again they show indiscriminacy, and shattering identities.[11] It may be plausible, then, especially in view of the purposely reflective temper of the final two cantos, to see the imagery of contradiction therein as part of the subsequent process of reassessment and recognition. It challenges our confidence in our reactions, laying bare the simplifications and prematurities which make experience regular at the expense of ignoring an ever-present fluidity or ambivalence. Byron accuses us, and Keats would have borne him a clear second, of binding ourselves and calling "some mode the best one" (*DJ* xiv.ii), even when "System" boils down to a perversion of the unnatural: it "doth reverse the Titan's breakfast" (*ibid.*). In this light it would be appropriate to turn to the poem not for the massive stability that absorbs the bombardment of details, but the un-

[11] See, for example, i.xxix, xxxiv, xli, lxxi; ii.xxiii, xliv, lvii-lix.

dazzled and unwearied reorientation that takes them as they come.

Mazeppa is as much given to action as Childe Harold to rumination; his aphorism (1. 524) and his philoso-phizing (ll. 718ff.) are barely removed from practical experience of what suffering does to the "bold" or of how the prospect of death affects various classes of men, and so belong to a different order from Childe Harold's con-siderations of time, knowledge, heroism, nature, etc. Where the peculiarities of imagery in *Childe Harold* might conceivably be suspected of artificiality, those same peculiarities in "Mazeppa" can only come of nat-uralism, expressing a personal impulse to describe and relate, with relatively little of the abstract purpose to an-alyze and define. The forms of experience in "Mazeppa" justify the formulations of the intellect in *Childe Harold*.

A pattern of unpredictability, summarized in the ques-tion "What mortal his own doom may guess?," is promi-nent in "Mazeppa," notwithstanding its quasi-allegorical use of space. "Will" and "guide"—internal and external promoters of our purposes—work incongruously, if they work. Between Charles and Casimir, contrasting kings, neither fortune nor reason seems to secure a choice, so that the fate of kingdoms as well as of persons appears somehow impenetrable. Mazeppa's experience proves wholly congruous with such a framework. The concealed social anomaly of the love between page and countess[12] foreshadows—I do not think it precipitates—a world in which even perception has no guarantee. From the mo-ment the cuckolded Count calls for "the horse" as if it

---

[12] Byron energetically attracts our attention to the anomaly with an oxymoron: "The happy *page*, who was the *lord* / Of one soft heart" (italics added).

were a fixed instrument of torture like the rack, the canons of expectation prove idle, and there is an increasing resort to imagery to handle the demands of actuality. The animal is likened to a torrent (1. 374), and to a meteor (1. 426), to a mountain-roe (1. 511),[13] to snow (1. 512), to a frustrated child (ll. 518-519), and to a wilful woman (ll. 519-520). All these images clearly share a common object of conveying driving energy and motion, though the last two seem concerned more with its emotional source than with its physical form; it is equally clear that no two chime together perfectly even in terms of energy and motion, so that we seem to witness the conflict of collaborating objects. Oppositions among the first four images are perhaps most numerous, but their ultimate value seems to depend on the child-woman images, which with their almost mathematical arrangement have been set up for special consideration: "Untired, untamed, and worse than wild— / All furious as a favoured child / Balked of its wish; or—fiercer still— / A woman piqued—who has her will!" Not only do these lines come at the end of a section, but they serve at once to re-open and to culminate the aforementioned series of images. More important yet, they show Byron purposefully revising his metaphor ("or fiercer still") without eliminating an antithesis, and offering something beyond, and not instead of, what has been given before. The affluence of images presents a series of perspectives

---

[13] There are some intriguing reminiscences between the present narrative time and the remembered vital time of the tale. This comparison of wild horse and roe has been anticipated in that of steed and fawn in ll. 76-77. Byron's control of context proves more than adroit enough to keep a basic distinction clear—the metaphor indicates docility in one case, and wild tirelessness in the other; the imagery of contradiction is compounded here.

as a sort of cubist unity to the eye, but for the mind. The limitations of the eye, in fact, lead to a strange effect, as the final images tend to make the response to the horse human as well as logical. The child in a tantrum and the woman with the upper hand all but defy visualization in terms of the horse; the reader is tempted to think he is learning what certain people as well as a certain horse may be like. But this counts less than the penetration into Mazeppa's mind through witnessing his continual effort to portray his horse and his ride. It is a mind grappling with the actuality of the senses with a competence hardly superior to that of the fastened body: Mazeppa in the one experience finds the inorganic, the organic, and the human, summer and winter, fire and water, the earthly and the celestial, the horizontal and the vertical, flowing and piling. Implicitly he has found a paradoxical definition of the possibilities of experience, in what could stand as the Byronic version of Wordsworth's mysteries of the known.

In the end Mazeppa's images for the borderland between self-possession and exhausted insensibility, having the same mixed character as those for his ride (ll. 544-560), may seem to intimate that he has been deranged all along. But any such impression is dispelled with the observation that he fetches the analogy for delirium from plain everyday experience of waves which "at the same time upheave and whelm." He even takes it for granted that the reader ("thee") is acquainted with the phenomenon, and can thereby gain access to the extraordinary world.[14] The vocabulary of the tale, moreover, bears

[14] If the shipwreck seems a somewhat infrequent and hence contrived occasion for the comparison, we may recall Byron's demonstration of the self-contradictions of anyone's experience, involving cases of simultaneous "scorching and drenching": "Did

pervasive witness to the difficult points of identity between distinct beings and states. A herd of horses in the forest is called a "troop" and a "squadron," with surprising associations with military regimentation, and then startlingly termed "the wild" and "the free." The word "wild" is used differently here than in numerous instances concerning the original horse of vengeance, and we further find both words, "wild" and "free," used of the eyes of the Cossack maid whom Mazeppa first sees upon his recovery of consciousness in human habitation and care. Other information is forthcoming, for example, about the maiden's eyes, but that too can cause a start—the wild and free eyes look "bright" and "gentle"! In short, not only is "wild" in itself a complex term, but it is used of complex subjects. The horses band together in an orderly way, even having "a patriarch of their breed," though they are not subject to any rational discipline; the girl is compassionate and generous, though not motivated by custom or prescription; the burdened horse heeds nothing but its own desires and impulses, which have been exacerbated with fury and fright into the further wildness that makes a "faint and low" voice "a sudden trumpet's clang" (ll. 456-459).

Mazeppa obviously feels a certain respect or affection for each of these "wild" things, but his very use of the word tends to stamp him as an observer of the forms— he is certainly punctilious as an old warrior in the care of his horse, and he seems to have been amazed, in the

---

he never spill a dish of tea over himself . . . ? Did he never swim in the sea at Noonday with the sun in his eyes and on his head, which all the foam of Ocean could not cool? Did he never draw his foot out of a tub of too hot water . . . ? Was he ever [becoming rhetorical and mischievous] in a cauldron of boiling oil?" (*LJ*, iv, 341-342).

midst of his youthful ordeal, at the natural sight of "a thousand horse—and none to ride!" The unconventional peculiarities of his imagery thus seem not just impressive, but ineluctable. And if we consider the implications of his struggle with imagery as well as the obvious facts that he is reliving, and not just relating the events of his past, we may infer a psychological pressure, a sort of narrative compulsion as a major feature of his performance. The tale will be told, once begun; and if there is humor in its being told in part to a sleeping audience, this humor is not without a strong tinge of poignancy. The episode of his ride becomes in a way analogous to the voyage of the Ancient Mariner, though Mazeppa's story is triggered from without, not from within, as only befits one who has turned into a grizzled soldier instead of a weird prophetic figure.

The narrator of *Don Juan* is too self-conscious and analytical for naturalism, and too much of an empiricist for orthodoxy, but finds use for the same sort of polyform imagery as Mazeppa. This has the initial advantage of seeming most apt to his easy-going, onward, excursive manner of speech. It goes deeper, and means more than that. No easy consistency, no protected schematization of imagery or otherwise goes by him unscanned or unscathed; his garrulity and levity, insistent enough in themselves, are mounted with barbs of agnostic opinion occasionally honed into aphorism. He is never dogmatic, but he is somehow portentous. His agnosticism ("such things are, which I can not explain," iii.xlvii) has deep roots in his character and every encouragement not only from everyday events: "the Fates / Change horses [with the moon], / Leaving at last not much besides chronology" (xiv.ciii), but also from the experimental

world of science: "What opposite discoveries we have
seen" (I.cxxix). It is hardly fortuitous that changes and
oppositions in imagery fairly abound in the expanse of
Don Juan. If they do not dominate the poem's fabric,
they are stitched into it with remarkable deftness, over-
lapping with each other and even picking up threads of
allusion for special effects.

We find Juan and Haidee both likened to birds (II.clxviii
and cxc), but for quite distinct and even conflicting relations of protector to pet and mate to mate. And such
rapid adaptation of the guise under which a particular
image operates confronts the reader often enough to
suggest that generalizations concerning a given image
or category of imagery must yield place to continual
discriminations within categories as a critical response
to Byron's method and design. The bird imagery of the
Haidee episode, in fact, is less striking in its frequency
than in the variety of its uses. In IV.xiv, though the idea
of mates does occur, Byron presents the bird to embody
not a kind of practical domestic relationship between two
people, but a mystical oneness based on intuition, and
foregoing it would seem both language and sense experience. Shortly again, in IV.xix, an analogy with the
loves of nightingales and doves suggests naturalistic
spontaneity and simplicity. If, however, these can all be
seen as favorable, appealing uses of the "bird imagery,"
giving Juan and Haidee a positive stature and luster,
they do not long go unqualified. In the end Byron virtually recants, with a twist of the bird imagery, what
that imagery has seemed to say. Falling into a subjunctive
mood, he makes use of the conception of a bird to tell us
what Juan and Haidee are not, and so cannot do: "They

should have lived together deep in woods, / Unseen as sings the nightingale . . ." (iv.xxviii).

The image of the lily, also used of both Juan and Haidee, appears less troublesome, since the two of them come before us in similar extremities (ii.cx and iv.lix), and since the image varies in accordance with who is looking (ii.xc and clxxvi) or what is being looked at (iii. lxxvi and iv.lxx). But a series of Biblical allusions enters and perplexes the case of the lily and the bird alike. The "lily" Juan has been "providentially" washed up on the island shore (ii.cvii) and Haidee has "cheered him both / With food and raiment" (cxxiii), deeming herself bound "'to take him in, / A stranger'" (cxxix). We are made mindful of a benevolent order of nature, and within that of a specifically Christian charity.

> And he said unto his disciples, Therefore I say unto you, Be not anxious for *your* life, what ye shall eat; nor yet for your body, what ye shall put on. For the life is more than the food, and the body than the raiment. Consider the ravens, that they sow not, neither reap; which have no store-chambers nor barn; and God feedeth them: of how much more value are ye than the birds! . . . Consider the lilies, how they grow: they toil not, neither do they spin; yet I say unto you, Even Solomon in all his glory was not arrayed like one of these.
>
> (Luke 12. 22-27; American Standard Version)[15]

But this order proves at best idle when Haidee is the "lily." Unlike the barely breathing Juan, with his largely bodily needs, she is in a situation transcending questions

---

[15] An extensive list of Biblical allusions in the Byron corpus is to be found in Arthur Pönitz, *Byron und die Bibel*, Leipzig, 1906.

of material self-preservation: "Food she refused, and raiment" (iv.lxviii). And Byron, pointedly telling us she "wither'd" (lxix, lxx) forces us to behold the violation of the order of happiness: "In vain the dews of Heaven descend above / The bleeding flower and blasted fruit of love" (lxx).

It seems unlikely that Byron is impugning the Christian scheme here; Haidee incarnates it even though her total experience does not fall neatly in its scope. The Christian scheme is portrayed as best, but not commonest.[16] His concern with the empirical order of circumstance, "that unspiritual god / And miscreator" (*CH* iv.cxxv) requires Byron to include what is inimical to the order of perfection, and also to admit its presence within that very order. Thus Haidee, if she is "lily" and "bird," is also something antipathetic to them, "snake," in the special way of one "who pours his length, / And hurls at once his venom and his strength" (ii.cxvii)—within perfection resides the quality of self-destruction, or as Blackstone cryptically puts it, "innocence is its own deepest guilt" (*The Lost Travellers*, p. 203). In addition there are those who on whatever grounds oppose perfection, such as Lambro, the "snake" that destroys not itself but others (iii.xlviii, iv.xlviii). Here again, however, the clear distinction in imagery is overlaid and largely overborne by the implied fact that Haidee defends Juan in part as a mother (ii.cliii, clviii), while Lambro attacks him (and to that extent Haidee herself!) with the parental instincts of the "cubless tigress" (ii.lviii).[17] And finally the

[16] Byron's dispraise of the distortions and petrifactions of Christian ideals and practice is eloquently treated by C. N. Stavrou in his article on "Religion in Byron's *Don Juan*" *SEL*, iii (1963), 567-594.

[17] Byron reaffirms the instinctive, incontrovertible force of

text hums with the continual reminder that time opposes perfection; it is riddled with forebodings (e.g. II.clxii, clxxiii, clxxxviii, cxcii; III.l, lxv; IV.viii-ix, xv, xxii-xxiv, xxx-xxxv).[18] No wonder that the narrator calls himself Cassandra (IV.lii).

Ultimately time and circumstances seem more to blame than Lambro, for whom Byron evidently has ambivalent feelings. Allusions to *The Odyssey* make this quite plain. We could think Juan is like Odysseus when he is washed ashore, but it would have to be conceded that Byron hardly highlights this possibility (II.cvii-cx).[19] It is certain, however, that he is thinking of Odysseus when Lambro makes his appearance (III.xxii-xxiii, li, lii); we are obliged to think of Lambro as a man and paterfamilias flagrantly wronged. "The notable lack of hostility toward Lambro" is ultimately explained by an ineradicable sense of this experience of wrong, and not just "by the fact that Byron is simply assuming that of course he *would* act as he does" (Ridenour, p. 83). Byron accounts clearly for any such assumption by the powerful allusion to Odysseus. That this comparison in the final analysis fails wholly to vindicate his conduct

---

mother love in the harem episode (v.cxxxii-cxxxiii); the strength of these statements puts the conduct of the calculating, formal mother, Donna Inez, in an even more unfavorable light.

[18] As the fatal moment in the fourth canto draws nearer, the omens crowd together with heightened urgency: an adept touch on Byron's part.

[19] Brian Wilkie, in his study of *Romantic Poets and Epic Tradition*, points out allusions to Homer's and to Dante's Ulysses at earlier stages of the shipwreck episode (Madison and Milwaukee, 1965, pp. 204-205); and Karl Kroeber and Bernard Blackstone, who both undiscriminatingly accept the Edenic overtones of Haidee's island life, observe that Byron compares Lambro to Ulysses on his return home (respectively, *Romantic Narrative Art*, Madison, Wisconsin, 1960, p. 157, and *The Lost Travellers*, p. 207).

and damns Haidee's as little as it does depends on the way Byron shifts the focus in mid-allusion, making Lambro "the Cyclops" (lvii), and making Haidee, in the midst of impious artificiality and luxury, as "pure as Psyche ere she grew a wife" (lxxiv). It would be hard to show everyone in the right, or in the wrong, on the strength of Byron's kaleidoscope of images and allusions. Indeed, Haidee seems as unimaginable without Lambro as he is inhuman without her. What the images and allusions imply is an oddly prolific world engendering more than it can reconcile or maintain. Its undeniable moments of splendor—Juan in shipwreck, Haidee in love, and, later, the Tartar Khan in battle—have no patent, but it is well to remember that we see them intimately before the telescope wheels us to the more inclusive view, and that the turns of the rhetoric are at once the narrator's practice and his obligation. He knows he is going to surprise, knows he is going to laugh before we do, but he too knows the poignancy of the mutable:

> And if I laugh at any mortal thing,
> 'T is that I may not weep. . . .
> (iv.iv)

As of the writing of *Childe Harold* iv (1817-18) it is possible to recognize as a hallmark of Byron's poetry a certain "meditative" or "contemplative"[20] response to the content of experience and to the weight of mutability and mortality therein. The way he presents dreams of destruction furnishes a fair idea of the change. An obsessive nightmare of all-annihilating death batters into the reader's consciousness in "Darkness" (1816), but the

[20] Byron's own words in this final canto, sts. xix, xxv, lxxvi, cxxviii, clvii, clviii.

poem suffers from the great disability of a nightmare, that it is a dissociated phenomenon which, if momentarily compelling, will soon be found wanting in substance. Certainly the "Darkness" that is "the Universe" in Byron's piece bears no comparison with Pope's "Universal Darkness," and largely because it has something merely arbitrary and external about it as corresponding to one man's isolated depression and not to an artistically, philosophically established state of things.[21] Two later nightmares of time show a clear gain in comprehensiveness, and in real power. Haidee's nightmare of the future in *Don Juan* IV.xcix (1819) and the hero's nightmare of the past in *Sardanapalus* IV.i (1821) have all the immediacy with none of the insularity of "Darkness," being designed as salient foci in a conceptual, and dramatic, and psychological frame of obvious complexity.

Both these nightmares strengthen characterization and thematic aims in the respective works. We know Haidee's nature, in the peculiar terms of the poem, much better than we know her thoughts. But her strongest assertion of her nature, that defiant challenge levelled at Lambro: "I knew / Your nature's firmness—know your daughter's too," emphatically reminds us that her parsimony with words coexists with a full apprehension of what she is and in what circumstances. Her life of bright harmonious instinct rests on clear deliberate principle—she *knew*. And her nightmarish sleep tells us more completely than anything else the gist of what she knew, namely, how harsh and hurtful a version of the Juan episode resided in the normal play of the conditions of her life. There is

[21] A more favorable view of Byron's poem as a "visionary lyric" is presented by Karl Kroeber in his study of *Romantic Narrative Art*, and in more general terms of poetic power by Blackstone in *The Lost Travellers*.

more wistful hope than conviction in her claim that Lambro "will forgive" her and Juan (iv.xxxviii). What at last can she mean in stating that she knew her father's nature? Is it inquisiturient to wonder whether Lambro has *always* held her in the shelter, in the chains of a paternal puritanism? Has Haidee as well as Juan stumbled into an interlude of love and grace? Certainly there may be doubt whether Lambro has, or could have left "the violence of his nature and his life" whenever his foot touched shore, whether "a kind of ideal life" has ever been "made possible by this violence" (Ridenour, p. 45). Her nightmare, revealing enough in itself, reacts intriguingly with other facets of the text.

The nightmare of Sardanapalus does not, like Haidee's, break through a cover of silence, but a cover of speech. Easy and articulate, Sardanapalus succeeds in keeping from himself no less than from us an inner sense of discomfort and danger under the downward burden of time, until its grotesque manifestation in his dream. The dynamism of the dream, significantly, carries the king, who will in reality compromise with his pacifist and hedonistic views, within range of reconciliation with his ancestors. The reconciliation fails, but the manner of failure still leaves Sardanapalus more closely bound to his past than before: he wishes in vain to maintain contact with the "hero" Nimrod, and wishes, again in vain, to break contact with the "crone" Semiramis. The nightmare, then, lays bare not just the unsuspected dimension, inside Sardanapalus, of his struggle against the set rhythms of society and history, but also an unsuspected ambivalence in that struggle. The implied failure of all the available options, to continue in his adopted course, to adhere to Nimrod, and to repudiate Semiramis may further remind us that Byron usually appears more pessimistic about the individual in history than about institutions. In *Sardanapalus* Byron most graphically shows his sense of "that dark compulsion that binds the race to its habitual conflicts."[22]

The enriched reverberations of the later nightmares in *Don Juan* and *Sardanapalus* as against that of *Darkness* fairly reflect an overall gain in power for Byron, and in particular show a capacity for condensed psychological dramatization that handsomely balances his more discursive vein. Yet it is not unlikely that the discursive vein provided the life-blood of such dramatic moments; the dramas are weakest not in conflict or dialogue, but in thematic comprehension and exactness. Great emphasis must be laid on the fact that apparent confusion in his work results from an extraordinary accuracy in rendering the simultaneity of plural states. Critics have seen this more readily in local passages than in Byron's writing at large, and have taken it as a random occurrence when it is a keynote of Byron's style. With the reservation that the stanza is typical, not "curious," I would like to quote Ridenour's impeccable analysis of this technique in *Don Juan* vii.xliii, for convenience first giving the lines:

> They fell as thick as harvests beneath hail,
> Grass before scythes, or corn below the sickle,
> Proving that trite old truth, that life's as frail
> As any other boon for which men stickle.
> The Turkish batteries thrash'd them like a flail,
> Or a good boxer, into a sad pickle
> Putting the very bravest, who were knock'd
> Upon the head, before their guns were cock'd.

[22] G. Wilson Knight, *The Starlit Dome*, London, 1941, p. 91.

Now Ridenour:

> The first line by itself could easily be taken
> 'straight.' There is nothing overtly humorous about
> it. But the two variants in the introductory simile
> provided by the second line make us feel less se-
> cure. There is suddenly something unnerving about
> this cold-blooded toying with images of violent
> death. We cannot react as we would, say, to a de-
> veloped Homeric simile using the same tenor and
> vehicle. This feeling is only increased by the off-
> hand cynicism of lines 3-4 and the flippant ver-
> sions of the simile in 5-6. . . . But at the same time
> we are aware of something else, of pity for them
> simply as men taking a beating, a pity controlled
> but not negated by the passages of superficial
> cynicism.
>
> (*Style*, pp. 72-73)

It is in the light of Byron's ever more frequent production of such chords of effortlessly controlled atonal-
ity that it becomes fitting to dwell on the analytical
strength and range of *Childe Harold* IV. In place of the
feverish and futile race for "transcendence rather than
. . . analysis of the Self" which Marshall sees in *Childe
Harold* III,[23] Byron in the concluding canto is by and
large reconciled to his own person (that would make
an important, if inconspicuous reason for his abandoning the tortuous, faint line between Harold and himself)
—and hence *less insistent on it*. He speaks in his own
person, but he speaks less self-consciously and more
humanely. Not that self-centered remarks altogether dis-

[23] *The Structure of Byron's Major Poems*, Philadelphia, 1962,
p. 74.

appear. One of Byron's most strident vauntings occupies a place in this canto (cxxxi ff.). But there is a curious duality in his outburst, which is in part meant for a profession of forgiveness and love, of full human harmony in the self; and besides, the stanzas on the singular speaker are clearly shown as eccentric (xxv, cxxxiv). One senses here a desperate reactive rush to fill the vacuum created by the removal of hostility. But the act of compensation entails its own turbulence, and as Marshall astutely indicates in the case of "The Prophecy of Dante," does not lend itself to the simplicity of a sudden affirmation: "The recognition of his vindictiveness is for the speaker the real beginning of his purge of . . . hatred and of his *ascent toward* positive affirmation. Psychologically, however, the loss of such an emotional force as the hatred itself, albeit negative, leaves him for the moment extremely close to despair" (*The Structure*, p. 129; italics added). Perhaps, though, "despair" does not quite fit the case. Like Byron in *Childe Harold* IV, Dante goes on to express an overweening expectation of his status before posterity, betraying withal some residue of antagonism in forecasting God's corrective rod on those who have trespassed against him. In like manner, in the "curse" of forgiveness, as Rutherford penetratingly says, we perceive not "genuine emotional or spiritual change, but rather . . . continued self-approval" (*Byron: A Critical Study*, pp. 94-95). The only likely extenuation is offered by G. Wilson Knight, to wit, that Byron "is cursing, as it were, through tears" (*Byron and Shakespeare*, p. 202).

The "meditative" method of *Childe Harold* IV, locally spotlighted in the key recognition of the "developing" nature of things (xxxiii, cxliii, clxi), and of the corresponding fact that "Our outward sense is but of gradual grasp" (see sts. clvii-clviii), projects itself at once in the arrangement of the opening stanzas. The dramatic first lines focus on the narrator less for himself than for his presence at a geographical and temporal vantage point from which to come to terms with the complex length of human history, whether cultural, political, or biographical; the latter category of course includes his own life. Significantly he begins by proposing to himself certain basic structural norms, in a sequence which could be supposed to follow a typical life-pattern. The first is imagination, or "beings of the mind" (v). The second, "strong reality" (vi), is virtually the converse of the first, and is made up of the special class of things which penetrate the mind from without, filling it with *their* existence instead of its own notions. Neither of these appealing possibilities wins final approval, though Byron brings them back for elaboration in terms of Art, and of Empire and Nature respectively, thus incidentally making Art and Nature important foci but not, as sometimes claimed, the final concerns of the canto. What he puts before both arbitrary predominance of the mind and its waxen docility is a new life designated as "waking Reason" (vii). This is unrelated to classical Reason, with its assumption and promotion of a strict universe of clear rule, order, and harmony; like the Wordsworthian Imagination, it is progressively cognitive and conceptual, but it precludes the *teleology* of Wordsworth's gift, relying on that discriminating totality of awareness which exacts poise rather than producing ecstasy in the possessor.

The mood associated with "waking Reason" is one of nearly stoical resignation (x, xxi), a spiritual condition which requires positive achievement and thus must be distinguished from earlier Childe-ish jadedness or apathy. The poem confronts the radical problem of reconciling the ubiquitous evidence of degeneration and death with the periodic manifestations of things whose perpetuation we would desire. In its first major phase, up to the middle of stanza lxi, Byron considers Empire and Art, and sees, in spite of the obvious losses to time, outstanding possibilities of survival—here "dust . . . is / Even itself an immortality" (liv). The section on Nature which follows (lxi.5-lxxvii) cites certain consolations, such as the fact that nature yields a "suspension of disgust" (lxviii), but it stresses human ineffectualness, the sure death of "fragile . . . clay."

There is a chiasmic reversal of these attitudes in the succeeding stanzas (lxix-cxxx), which deal with Empire, Art and Nature all together, as elements of a more basic consideration of the possibilities of knowledge. Thus at first general fragility and incertitude are projected, most graphically perhaps in the passage on Metella: "Thus much alone we know—Metella died, / The wealthiest Roman's wife. Behold his love or pride!" Pessimism is made explicit in the poem's initial summary of the meaning of history:

> There is the moral of all human tales:
> 'T is but the same rehearsal of the past
> First Freedom and then Glory—when that fails,
> Wealth, vice, corruption,—barbarism at last.
> And History, with all her volumes vast,
> Hath but *one* page. . . .
>   (cviii)

Such pessimism reaches its intensest force in the concluding stanza of the section, "Our life is a false nature . . ." (cxxvi). This is the nadir, the exaggeration of despair which "waking Reason" will not countenance, though it cannot utterly controvert it. The next brief phase (cxxvii-cxxx) qualifies despair by suggesting the possibility of a resolution, the possibility of light, making uncanny use of the Coliseum as a fused emblem of art, empire, and nature in deathless realization, and offering a more balanced conception of Time as "beautifier," "corrector," and "avenger." But of course it must be noted that the Coliseum passage redeems despair by qualification, instead of true affirmation. However ruefully, Byron is prepared to own that "the colossal fabric's form . . . will not bear the brightness of the day" (cxliii). It turns out, too, that some of his claims in the propitious moonlight really reflect the logic of his expectations ("for divine / Should be the light which streams here"), and tend to disregard what may be more important, his abiding conviction and his experience; and the way he frames the strange and moving scene where daughter nourishes father, with examples of impiety (Cain) and impropriety (Hadrian's "Mole"), sets off the excellence of her action at the cost of proposing a negative value for the generality of things that are given birth.

The chiasmic structure of the canto to this point[24] contains and stabilizes the very variation of mood which tends to produce weltering in *Childe Harold* III. This equilibrium, alike the product and the vindication of waking Reason, is more than formal of course. It reflects the narrator's accommodation with human experience, historically taken, just as that accommodation must

[24] For a more detailed picture of the organization of *Childe Harold* IV according to the sequence of single topics and subjects, the reader should consult Joseph's *Byron the Poet*, pp. 83ff.

underlie his proposal of reconciliation with living humankind (cxxxi-cxxxvii). The remainder of the canto apparently assumes that the new entente is unblemished and complete ("The seal is set.—Now welcome, thou dread power!", cxxxviii), but it repeats the difficulty Byron has with the immediate world, making his "curse" of "Forgiveness" seem a coercive conversion of terms.[25] Unlike that of the dying Gladiator or of Laocoön, his own suffering ultimately lacks the benefit of the critical perspective supplied by time or art. The mind that comes to terms with the fates of, say, Dante and Petrarch is too involved in the fresh fate of Princess Charlotte to handle it serenely. The magnificent human confidence of its identification with St. Peter's collapses, with the disappointment of the messianic hope in the Princess' expected child, into a gloom closely akin to the earlier state of despair; the image of the ill-omened "meteor" firmly links the two (clxx, cxxiv).

The conception of the single life as a bubble floating on, or sinking into the ocean, in youth and at death respectively (clxxxiv, clxxix), may seem the final dispassionate statement of the casual, and insubstantial quality of life; it is a picture of nature thinly tolerating then annihilating man and whatever is generated by him. But Byron's "prying into the abyss" has yielded him an undeniable, if not an unqualified composition of spirit. To add the character of Time the destroyer is not to recant all faith in the beautifier, the corrector. . . . One might seem, through what he himself calls the "loops of time,"

---

[25] Gleckner calls the idea of forgiveness "new and somewhat startling," and aptly points out that "in the original skeletal manuscript . . . the curse remained but a curse" (*Ruins*, p. 290). Byron has not so much revised or repudiated the curse as reinforced it with singularity.

to discern the means of escaping his indictment. The very griefs which mar his trembling resignation arise from no dishonorable weaknesses. He is capable, to the end, of at least a Lawrentian hope in nature (clxxvi-clxxvii), and also of recreating, as an inalienable intuition, that former contact with eternity when, with terrifyingly cautionless, charmed innocence, he rested his hand on the "mane" of the "dread, fathomless" ocean. And he is in possession of that intelligence with respect to the past which can declare mankind rid of an immemorial onus: "And if it be Prometheus stole from Heaven / The fire which we endure, it was repaid. . . ." In the final analysis, perhaps, the achievement of waking Reason is a chiaroscuro one, tempering and yet heightening pain, leading to praise and pride and then again to belittlement and dismay, settling our account with an archaic mythology but coming up short of a new frame of reference: the old benefit of fire cannot be dispensed with, and now is something "we endure." If, as Byron asserts, "we can recall . . . visions" of "brightest," godly moments, we end up only with "things" that "look like gods below." No special emphasis need be put on "below" to bring out an undertone of compromise and making-do in this resemblance to the divine.

Still it is hard to resolve whether the degree of failure offsets or sets off the partial success. *Childe Harold* IV announces and embodies a major new attitude, not a manifesto. Its "meditative" orientation does not demand solutions, but holds it necessary, proper, and cardinal to "ponder boldly" (cxxvii), so that the recognition of true problems becomes a substantial value, as does the accurate gauging of how, and how far a comprehensive conceptual scheme can be defended. Even at this point it would seem necessary to challenge the rather comprising summary of Byron's work and mind offered by Carlyle upon receiving the news of the poet's death: "Poor Byron! And but a young man; still struggling amid the perplexities, and sorrows, and aberrations, of a mind not arrived at maturity or settled in its proper place in life." Aside from the reflection that one man's maturity is another man's arrogance, Byron conjures up an empirical definition of one's proper place as where it is possible, all things considered, to be. Strictly speaking he is *grappling* with perplexities, not in a situation to be settled by any arbitrary number of falls, but as a root condition of existence. And *Childe Harold* IV thus takes on pivotal significance with its unflinching presentation of a mind that sacrifices tidiness to inclusiveness, a mind whose virtue it is to work *ex necessitate rei*, rather than ex cathedra.[26]

For all its lack of resolution, that mind attains a viable state in being at once personal and analytical, idealistic and undemanding, humble and uncompromising. In *Don Juan*, its position is duly expanded into a philosophy, and complemented with a full-fledged personality.

[26] Rutherford suggestively argues that in *Childe Harold* IV Byron's style is being modulated toward harmony with the *Don Juan* style (*Byron: A Critical Study*, pp. 100-101).

· V ·

A SAD JAR OF ATOMS?
ANTIDROMIC ORDER
IN *DON JUAN*

Unity is the cloke of folly. WILLIAM BLAKE

The unfurling canvas of *Don Juan*, while anything but
molded or taut, exhibits a ceaseless animation, a peculiar
energy not expressing the potential of form but *derived,*
chronically and somewhat conspicuously, from the story-
teller. The play of images in the poem makes a fair introduction to that energy at work; as we have seen, images
which might be thought to occur confusedly follow a
describable pattern and lead to the definite end of re-
cording the fluency and contrarieties of experience. The
ordained complexity of imagery in "The Destruction of
Sennacherib" (above, pp. 32-34)[1] is supplanted by a con-
glomerating imagery which, whether or not it is ever
substantially complete, discourages the placidity of a
predictable resolution. The cross-relations of imagery
in *Don Juan,* bearing as they do on the question of structure, conduce to a special kind of coherency that we will
see reinforced by a host of technical details in the poem.

---

[1] A variable grouping of images in "The Siege of Corinth,"
composed like the *Hebrew Melodies* in 1815, comes closer to
what I have called the imagery of contradiction. Byron presents
the attacking "Moslem multitude" consecutively in the guise of
marauding wolves, of shattering glass, and of levelled grass
(II.722-738). But he is dealing here with clearly distinct aspects
of the warriors' existence, their plans and attendant conduct,
their vulnerability, their insignificance in death. The series of
images seems fairly straightforward, so that to my mind the
epistemological resonance of the imagery of contradiction is hardly
perceptible.

The restless, uncoordinated movements virtually forced on Byron as he seeks to establish one or another distorting and infirm position, in *Childe Harold* III, get assimilated in *Don Juan* and elaborated into a paradoxical system which not only takes perplexity for granted but methodically fosters it.

The latter poem, as recent criticism has maintained, is amenable to treatment in various ways: as an elaboration of the theme of the Fall, with grace and reason decayed (Ridenour); or of the theme of appearance versus reality, entailing a satirical view of hypocrisy (Rutherford, Lovell, et al.); or again as an image of Byron's quicksilver personality and recurrent vision of some ideal (Hirsch). But it would appear that *Don Juan* is amenable to such interpretations only up to a point. Concerning the idea of a fall, the poem, which is capable of undercutting the purport of the Fall so far as to proclaim "man's worst—his *second* fall," seems but occasionally and obliquely interested in any of the theological (or even ethical) considerations always put among the foremost by those who have sung "Of Man's first disobedience." In point of fact Byron even eschews any indication of the context of the Fall, of the sort of practical occasion that might yield germane philosophical inferences. "How man *fell*," he explicitly confesses, "I / Know not" (*DJ* IX.lv).[2] He has contrived or conspired to keep enough of the cultural sense of the Fall to elicit a distinct emotional reaction to the evidence of man's imperfection, much as Milton makes poetic capital of a mythological

[2] Is it sheer mischief to see this reference to man's spiritual condition converted, reduced to a description of simple physiological, *organic* processes in the succeeding lines, where Byron, in connection with love (or lust), is so certain as to "how [man] *falls* and rises"? Certainly both belong to one postlapsarian state.

currency he is thematically devaluating (Hesperian fables true, if true, here only). For Byron effectively collapses the religious and moral propositions founded on that evidence; Ridenour states that the "art" of *Don Juan* is meant to abet "civilization in its struggle for 'the diminution of the traces of Original Sin,'" (*Style*, pp. 29-32), and sees in the Aurora Borealis passage in the poem evidence of a world "molded and illuminated by the sacramental power of imagination" (p. 95). But the material of the poem does not chime with such claims, as Ridenour seems to acknowledge where he contradicts them both. He calls *Don Juan* a "rather terrifying vision of a personal and cultural dead end" (xiii) and "an act of acquiescence in the real world," a world "which is, for the most part, simply given" (p. 123), and speaks of the charm Byron shows in the mere icy world earlier supposed to be transformed and revitalized by imagination (pp. 33, 122). *The Style of Don Juan*, often so acute in analysis and discerning in generalization, is also often crossed with such inexactness and inconsistency, and its impact correspondingly weakened. The study does not seem to accept and pursue as fully as it might the implications of its own perception that the Fall is a metaphor —indeed a metaphor of a metaphor—for Byron (p. 21),[3] in a world scheme where "the worlds of grace and of reason" have "largely slipped away" (p. 150). The way Byron interchanges and equates Lucifer, Prometheus, and Phaëthon as emblems of a fall essentially expresses

---

[3] How difficult its application can be appears graphically from Rutherford's contention that "Byron formulates . . . his own version of the Fortunate Fall—sin is more fun than innocence or virtue, and Man's life may be less pure now than it was in Eden, but it is also (as a consequence) far more enjoyable" (*Byron: A Critical Study*, p. 144).

the case, as the theological and prototypal (Lucifer) becomes identified with or narrowed down to the humanistic and mythical (Prometheus), and both suffer an equation with the empirical and merely mythological (Phaëthon). The idea of a fall enables Byron to talk about man as being imperfect, not as having become so; we see the "troubled stream" that is man, but get only empty claims of its having a "pure source" ("Prometheus"). The radical "uncertainty of . . . point of view" which Ridenour sees in Byron, if it is initially compatible with the lapsarian myth, must soon prove antagonistic to its basic beliefs, making "the categories of innocence and experience" substantially "irrelevant" (*Style*, p. 122).

This same uncertainty, or rather perhaps unassertiveness of viewpoint ultimately makes the theme of appearance vs. reality unacceptable as the overriding one in the poem. To Byron, when all is said and done, appearance is in reality, not opposed to it, and the reprehensible thing to suppress what is apparent in favor of what is convenient, to forge or follow necessarily dark tunnels through the mountains of appearing things to some desired haven. In short, while recognizing deceit and self-deceit in the matter of appearances, Byron would not seem sufficiently assured of the essential terms of "reality" to make it one of his key principles; one can see throughout *Don Juan* evidence of Byron's realizing "that the distinction between the appearance and reality is often not clear or at least cannot always be clearly drawn."[4] But obviously this does not make Byron indifferent to the task of marshalling and evaluating appearances, does not make him forego intellectual and artistic

[4] Edward E. Bostetter, *The Romantic Ventriloquists*, Seattle, 1963, p. 250.

direction in his magnum opus. The poem doubtless images Byron's personality, but it also embodies his thought; as Willis W. Pratt has contended, Byron seems to have had "a plan above and beyond presenting a panoramic and incisive picture of hypocrisy and cant."[5]

It has already been observed that Byron purposely fashions a degree of technical disorder to dramatize the epistemological dilemma of human experience, where at last, to invoke a telling children's song, the ascent of the mountain of experience leads to "the other side of the mountain." Byron, as will presently be seen, makes the whole of *Don Juan* a multiform statement of obligatory irresolution, in terms of "his own increasingly clear understanding of the limitations of human understanding" (Pratt, *ibid.*); but not without the most inveterate probing of reputed paths to resolution. One of these in particular warrants some discussion, in part because it has been overlooked in the sizable assembly of influences on *Don Juan,*[6] and more importantly because Byron himself proposed it and went out of his way to try it, though only to find it wanting. The influence, the ordering principle involved is that of Restoration comedy, and its final inefficacy will furnish a useful comment on the question of Byron's treatment of English society.

Casual comments Byron makes concerning his mature satires, and statements he makes within the compass of *Don Juan*, make it evident that he was conscious of working in the tradition of Congreve, Vanbrugh, and Far-

[5] "Byron and Some Current Patterns of Thought," in *The Major English Romantic Poets*, ed. C. D. Thorpe et al., Carbondale, Illinois, 1957, p. 158.

[6] See for example Elizabeth Boyd, *Byron's Don Juan: A Critical Study*, New Brunswick, New Jersey, 1945, and András Horn, *Byron's "Don Juan" and the Eighteenth Century English Novel*, Bern, Switzerland, 1962.

quhar. He is all but explicit about imitating Congreve in setting up the motley Cast of Characters at Norman Abbey (*DJ* xiii.lxxix ff.),[7] appearing both to protect himself from censure on the basis of Congreve's practice, and to censure the age for failing to keep it up:

> If all these seem an heterogeneous mass
> To be assembled at a country seat,
> Yet think, a specimen of every class
> Is better than a humdrum tête-à-tête.
> The days of Comedy are gone, alas!
> When Congreve's fool could vie with Molière's *bête*:
> Society is smoothed to that excess,
> That manners hardly differ more than dress.
> (*DJ* xiii.xciv)

The imitation of Congreve and appeal to his authority— the mention of Molière is more pedantic than significant —are all the more striking in that Byron troops his Congreve body of persons across the stage and then virtually forgets them. Judging by the way the poem proceeds, there seems to be little likelihood that Byron would have brought back more of the "heterogeneous mass" than he does. He is concerned, in the main narrative, with Lord Henry and Lady Adeline Amundeville, the Duchess of Fitz-Fulke, Aurora Raby, and his hero, Don Juan. The rest manifestly are introduced for two chief reasons: to do homage to Congreve, and in corollary, to analyse and rebuke that contemporary uniformity of "manners" and "dress" which he goes on to prove unnatural and untrustworthy. Interestingly enough, Goldsmith has taken a

---

[7] We may note here that Swinburne saw Julia, in her letter to Juan, as a "lineal descendant of Wycherley's Olivia in the *Plain Dealer*" ("Wordsworth and Byron," in *The Complete Works*, ed. Gosse and Wise, London, 1926, xiv, 177).

similar view of upperclass "style" in *An Enquiry into the Present State of Polite Learning in Europe*:

> Does the poet paint the absurdities of the vulgar, then he is *low*; does he exaggerate the features of folly to render it more thoroughly ridiculous, he is then very *low*. In short, they have proscribed the comic or satirical muse from every walk but high life, which, though abounding in fools as well as the humblest station, is by no means so fruitful in absurdity. Among well-bred fools we may despise much, but have little to laugh at; nature seems to present us with a universal blank of silk, ribbons, smiles, whispers.

In relation to the question of uniformity, Strongbow and Longbow are particularly noteworthy. As the rhyme of their names suggests, they are akin, and yet distinct. Strongbow and Longbow are "wits," a detail of some significance where Byron has Congreve in mind. Of even greater significance is the difference between them as wits. The following is Byron's description:

> There also were two wits by acclamation,
> Longbow from Ireland, Strongbow from
> $\qquad$ the Tweed—
> Both lawyers and both men of education—
> But Strongbow's wit was of more polished breed;
> Longbow was rich in an imagination
> As beautiful and bounding as a steed,
> But sometimes stumbling over a potato,—
> While Strongbow's best things might have
> $\qquad$ come from Cato.

Strongbow was like a new-tuned harpsichord;
But Longbow wild as an Aeolian harp,
With which the Winds of heaven can claim accord,
And make a music, whether flat or sharp.
Of Strongbow's talk you would not
                               change a word:
At Longbow's phrases you might sometimes carp:
Both wits, one born so, and the other bred—
This by his heart—his rival by his head.

Of course Strongbow has been identified as John Philpot Curran, and Longbow as Thomas Lord Erskine, but still we may see in the way Byron opposes them, in what is avowedly a Congrevian context, a modified version of the typical Restoration playing-off of the false wit against the true, the natural against the affected.

Recognitions of the fact that Byron is conceiving of "that Microcosm on stilts, / Yclept the Great World" (XII.lvi) in direct relation to the Restoration helps to clarify a cryptic statement he makes early in the cantos on England. He is deploring the disingenuousness of people "Who like to play the fool with circumspection" (XI.lxxi), and abruptly bursts into an apostrophe of a former fashion:

> . . . If you can contrive, get next at supper;
> Or, if forestalled, get opposite and ogle:—
> Oh, ye ambrosial moments! always upper
> In mind, a sort of sentimental bogle,
> Which sits for ever upon Memory's crupper,
> The ghost of vanished pleasure once in vogue!

It would appear probable that Byron imagined the Restoration as the time when those ambrosial moments, those pleasures were openly in vogue.

From the very start Byron discussed *Don Juan* in terms which implicitly ranked it alongside Restoration comedy. He wonders, in a spirit of roguish irony, whether the "quietly facetious" poem—yet unpublished—"is not . . . too free for these very modest days" (*LJ*, iv, 260). Earlier, after seeing *The Trip to Scarborough*, Sheridan's close adaptation of Vanbrugh's *The Relapse*, he had anticipated the gist of such a comment: "Congreve and Vanbrugh are your only comedy. Our society is too insipid now for the like copy" (*LJ*, ii, 398). The conception of a sophisticated sort of comedy as giving offense to a modest, or insipid, society is only too clear in both quotations. The correspondence may fairly be taken to be more than chance, and merits particular emphasis in that it tends to show Byron thinking of the first, as of the last, cantos in connection with the Restoration.

Another correspondence between Byron's description of *Don Juan* and of Restoration comedy should also be noted. He declares that "the comedies of Congreve, Vanbrugh, Farquhar, Cibber, etc., . . . naturally attempted to represent the manners and conversation of private life" (*LJ*, v, 574). He says essentially the same thing of the cantos on England, telling us he deals with "Knights and Dames. . . , / Such as the times may furnish," and confessing "the difficulty" of "colouring / With Nature manners which are artificial" (xv.xxv).

General ways in which *Don Juan* reflects Restoration influence are readily perceived. Byron's poem is racy and cynical, emphasizing, as Ridenour says, a worldly and sophisticated point of view (*The Style of Don Juan*, p. 120), embodying an amorality that yet admits of a retracted satire. It avoids, though Byron boasts of his variety—"A slight glance thrown on men of every station"—what is rural and lowly, or converts it into worldly terms, so that Lambro is a "great . . . loss to good society," the highwayman is a Prime Minister *manqué*, and the scene in the harem fit for a Restoration comedy. Even the underlying skepticism of *Don Juan* has its counterpart in Restoration comedy—one justification of "the mode" was that "the spouseless virgin *Knowledge* flies," that, as Socrates avers, nothing can be known. Indeed, both Congreve, in the first scene of *The Old Bachelor*, and Byron in *Don Juan* (vii.v), specifically cite the agnosticism of the Greek sage.

The general treatment of sex and marriage in *Don Juan* could, of course, easily remind one of Restoration comedy, for Byron displays at once Etherege's graceful insouciance, Congreve's practical idealism, and Wycherley's combination of hanky-panky and puritanism. But a sounder claim may be made for special points of similarity, where Byron's statements have the mold and ring of the Restoration. In a brilliantly condensed epigram Byron writes: "A rib's a thorn in a wed gallant's side" (xi.xlvi). And one recalls a couplet from Congreve's *The Old Bachelor*, which also includes the metaphor of calling a wife a rib and the equation of wedded misery and physical pain: "And Adam, sure, could with more ease abide, / The bone when broken, than when made a bride" (v.iv). A sardonic view of marriage pervades *Don Juan*, and it is not surprising to hear Byron again sounding like Congreve at his best: "Marriage from Love, like vinegar from wine" (iii.v). One wonders if Byron could have extrapolated from Restoration comedy the skeptical view that "All comedies are ended by a marriage" (III.ix). And finally one personage in *Don Juan* comes to mind, the Empress Catherine whose imperious carnality is virtually a summation of all the relentless middle-aged female lasciviousness of Restoration comedy. She is Lady Wishfort with a difference; her wish is a command.

For all of this it would seem that Restoration matter has been dissolved into *Don Juan*, noticeably coloring it perhaps, but not much more; certainly not even the English books of *Don Juan* have been crystallized in a Restoration manner. An explanation can be offered in terms of the exigencies of form: if not absolutely in terms of the difference between drama and narrative, then in terms of the peculiar discursive method of narration to which Byron resorts. For Byron is concerned with more than manners, but less than morals. The manners of the Amundevilles prove more successful as a compromise with circumstances than to satisfy the liberal in nature; the morals of "her frolic Grace, Fitz-Fulke" are made less reprehensible than to content the illiberal in spirit. In between what we do and what we are Byron focuses on what we know; the characterization of the two ladies in question is permeated with epistemological issues, not the least intriguing of which is the impasse of values whereby it becomes impossible to take Lady Amundeville, with her frigidity, over the Duchess Fitz-Fulke, with her lubricity; or vice versa.

That Byron by and large fails to make good on his threat to show a fundamental Restoration line in contemporary life suggests neither the conclusion that his vision was inaccurate nor that his form was recalcitrant.[8]

[8] As regards the charge of inaccuracy, see especially Edward Dudley Hume Johnson, "Don Juan in England," *ELH*, XI (1944),

His strictly social concerns, which enable him to use and in a way revive the Restoration mode, are but ancillary to his epistemological concerns, which oblige him to go beyond that mode. And the same will be found true of other influences on *Don Juan*, like the eighteenth-century novel, for example, or classical comedy or Italian comic verse, or as will shortly be shown, of satirical and epic tradition.

The bounty of particular, one might even say local, themes and subjects and considerations in *Don Juan* (and even unsympathetic critics recognize "the poet's inexhaustible mind")[9] needs finally to be seen as the eclectic instruments of a primary impulse to evolve a gospel of uncertainty. And propagate it, as the purest

---

135-153. The possibility of a recalcitrant form has hardly been studied in the present connection. Bostetter has suggested that Byron had "temporarily run out of inspiration" and did not "quite know how to get his narrative of English life under way" (*Ventriloquists*, p. 242). But he is arguing largely on the unsatisfactory assumption of a conventionally *narrative* organization in *Don Juan*. Ridenour has made the more positive, and more substantial suggestion that the English cantos are set up "in epic terms," representing the section of the poem where Byron "seems to be making his most earnest attempt at dramatizing the possibility of 'real Epic'" (*Style*, p. 111). This "most earnest attempt" proves if anything less successful than the quasi-Restoration format. Perhaps it is apropos to recall the admonition of George Santayana, in *Soliloquies in England*, concerning the irretrievability of past forms and the insecurity of present ones:

Substance is fluid, and since it cannot exist without some form, is always ready to exchange one form for another; but sometimes it falls into a settled rhythm or recognizable vortex, which we call a nature, and which sustains an interesting form for a season. These sustained forms are enshrined in memory and worshipped in moral philosophy, which often assigns to them a power to create and to reassert themselves that their precarious status is very far from justifying. But they are all in all to the mind: art and happiness lie in pouring and repouring the molten metal of existence through some such tenable mould.

[9] Davie, *Purity of Diction*, p. 131.

extract from the "facts," and the greatest expression of
the "truth." In that it makes such a feature of the poet's
(and the poem's) relation to the audience, *Don Juan*
might be taken for the great public poem of the inward-
oriented romantic period;[10] in fact it leads away from
public solidarity, public assent in the replenishment and
reconsecration of the public good, and aims toward a
state of disequilibrium, showing withal a humorous cool-
ness that eliminates for the reader the escape route of
shared indignation or lamentation customary in "pessimistic" romantic poems.[11] The author of *Don John* ar-
restingly suggests that *Don Juan* "wars with virtue, as
resolutely as with vice."[12] Certainly he is warring with
what is received as virtue by a concert of public opinion,
and warring against the sort of political definition of
truth quintessentially given by Martin Heidegger: "the
revelation of that which makes a people certain, clear,

[10] This viewpoint is implicit in Lovell's contention that *Don
Juan* revives the idea of a poem as "made for people other than
its creator" (*Irony and Image*, p. 230).

[11] The attempt to make the reader not only see but subscribe
to a philosophy of agnosticism must have given rise to much of the
instinctive resentment and aversion which Byron met from his
contemporaries over *Don Juan*. A strange intellectual and moral
insecurity is discernible in their strictures; and Francis Jeffrey, in
his impressively thoughtful article in the *Edinburgh Review*, enunciates a sharp sense of the danger that Byron's work might corrupt not only by wicked example but by wicked argument
("Lord Byron's Tragedies," xxxvi [1822], 448, 449). A more impersonal view is advanced by C. N. Stavrou, who terms Don Juan
"an earnest adjuration to men to desist from self-deception" ("Religion in Byron's *Don Juan*," SEL, III [1963], 593-594). Ernest
J. Lovell, Jr. enthusiastically sees the promotion of self-knowledge
and the lessening of self-deception as an unalloyed and incontestable proof of charity and idealism in *Don Juan*, something which
will "heal" the community (*Irony and Image*, p. 230). In principle
this may be so; but it is a principle which assumes greater access
to knowledge than *Don Juan* confesses, to say nothing of its disregard for the real trauma of unfamiliar truth.

[12] *'Don John' or Don Juan Unmasked*, London, 1819, p. 8.

and strong in its action and knowledge." Without realization of this constant principle of structure, this motive
for surprise and change, one is all too likely to conclude,
as Hazlitt does in *The Spirit of the Age*, that Byron's
"only object seems to be to stimulate himself and his
readers for the moment—to keep both alive, to drive
away ennui, to substitute a feverish and irritable state
of excitement for listless indolence or even calm
enjoyment."

But *Don Juan* stands as more than a thing of flashy
juxtapositions; it is created as a universe of the unpre-
dictable, containing, as Byron had once said of his mind,
"500 contradictory contemplations, though with but one
object in view" (*LJ*, III, 254). It abounds in untoward
developments, like *The Prelude*, but unlike that work results in no final, all-encompassing serenity. Conceding
nothing to the force of "that vice-nature, custom," Byron
advances before us with a "dedication" that is at best a
rebuke, and hardens into a denunciation; he promises
an epic which on inspection does not so much revise as
revoke the epic tradition. Here is a hero chosen by
default and on the strength of his popularity "in the pan-
tomime"; an ironic boast of "regularity" in design reck-
lessly set beside a confession of irregularity in going
against "the usual method"; an irreverently stingy and
belated invocation ("Hail, Muse! *et cetera*"); and continual notice that the writer, though he may "have a high
sense / Of Aristotle and the Rules," is proudly prone to
"err a bit." In part, we should observe, he is making
merry at the expense of epic as codified by a procrustean
criticism (III.cxi), but it is undeniable that the traditional "*épopée*" had internal shortcomings for him too
(III.xcvii).

· *141* ·

Byron's response to the convention of satire, if subtler, proves no less disruptive. He foregoes the satirist's traditional readiness, and responsibility, to speak with authority, projecting instead in his magnum opus that "uncertainty of . . . point of view" which accepts alike the limitations of satire and of judgment. Thus, as demonstrated by Ernest J. Lovell, Jr., one can argue at one point that Byron scores Donna Julia for her hypocrisy and fleshliness, and still go on to acknowledge uncertainty about his real attitude ("Irony and Image in *Don Juan*," pp. 232, 236-237). For Byron also gives up the satirist's selective tendency. He exhibits Donna Julia's faults with infallible accuracy, and her needs with unmistakable sympathy, or, as Ridenour says, "with quiet, tender mockery" (*Style*, p. 79). We see her, just the way we see Gulbeyaz and Lady Adeline, to cite two sharply dissimilar characters, as a person typifying certain vices, but also as a person suffering with and from her vices. Conversely, when Juan seems most resplendent and triumphant, in Catherine's court, his status is most dubious:

> Suppose him in a handsome uniform—
> A scarlet coat, black facings, a long plume,
> Waving, like sails, new shivered in a storm,
> Over a cocked hat in a crowded room,
> And brilliant breeches, bright as a Cairn Gorme,
> Of yellow cassimire we may presume,
> White stockings drawn uncurdled as new milk,
> O'er limbs whose symmetry set off the silk;
>
> Suppose him sword by side, and hat in hand,
> Made up by Youth, Fame, and an army tailor—
> The great enchanter, at whose rod's command

Beauty springs forth, and Nature's self turns paler,
Seeing how Art can make her work more grand
(When she don't pin men's limbs in like
           a gaoler),—
Behold him placed upon a pillar! He
Seems Love turned a Lieutenant of Artillery!

His bandage slipped down into a cravat—
His wings subdued to epaulettes—his quiver
Shrunk to a scabbard, with his arrows at
His side as a small sword, but sharp as ever—
His bow converted into a cocked hat—
But still so like, that Psyche were more clever
Than some wives (who make blunders no less stupid),
If she had not mistaken him for Cupid.
    (ix.xliii-xlv)

This is a dazzling picture, by which Juan virtually
becomes the god Cupid—he is subsequently also associated with Mercury, and even with the Sun (lxvi,
lxix). The picture, though it has been seen to exemplify
"mainly comic ingenuity and exuberance" (Joseph,
p. 218), has disturbing features, amounting to an apothe-
osis of clothes or at least of a man as his clothes, which
both stimulate and symbolize mere sex. The "divinized"
Juan can be seen as a fop transformed into an Object of
Love to serve the unabating lust of the Empress, whose
association with Messalina and Clytemnestra (lxxii, lxxx)
further undercuts his position. The end degrades the
means here, and the means is doubly degraded by its
source—the army tailor as enchanter. Though Byron will
call Don Juan "a full-grown Cupid" (xiv.xli), he counter-
balances such praise now with repeated suggestions that
we are viewing Cupid in decline: "Slipped down," "sub-

dued," "shrunk," "small." In the face of a simultaneous enlargement and contraction, a resolute reaction does not come easy; one cannot but demur at Ridenour's peremptory label: "a particularly repellent manifestation of the world of experience" (*Style*, p. 142). How does one forget that the enchanter is a tailor, or deny that the tailor is an enchanter? Without going so far as, Crabbewise, to suggest "how extremely improper it would be, by any allusion, however slight, to give any uneasinesss, however trivial, to any individual, however foolish or wicked,"[13] Byron does have Don Juan operating in a special world, in which the sensuous or aesthetic standard seizes the eye, and mind, to the cost of the moral standard.

It is a highly sophisticated world, and one should remember that it rests on a distinct philosophy which Byron makes quite explicit: "If I agree that what is, is;— then this I call / Being quite perspicuous and extremely fair" (xi.v).[14] Scrutiny comes before obedience, vigilant perceptiveness ranks above dogma. Though it will prove that Byron includes certain predilections and orthodoxies in the compass of "what is," he is so strongly disposed to mistrust strictly clean categories that the primary bent of his philosophy must be termed skeptical. He is "an Anychean, or Anything-arian."[15] Hence as a satirist he is

[13] Horatio and James Smith, *Rejected Addresses*, 3rd American edn., Boston, 1841, p. 128.

[14] This strangely modulated statement, at once amiable and controversial, positive and agnostic, can hardly escape being taken as a deliberate reminder and revision of Pope's neoclassical view; the assertion that "what is, is" amounts to a deft, direct subversion of the principle that "whatever is, is right."

[15] Thomas Medwin, *Conversations of Lord Byron*, ed. Ernest J. Lovell, Jr., Princeton, New Jersey, 1966, p. 80.

incongruously overcome by his "tendency to spare"
(IX.xxi), and has to confess:

My Muse, the butterfly hath but her wings,
Not stings, and flits through ether without aim,
Alighting rarely:—were she but a hornet,
Perhaps there might be vices which would mourn it.
(XIII.lxxxix)

A comparable outlook is found in *Beppo*, in wryly
apologetic lines that make a virtual manifesto for the
new Byronic satire:

I fear I have a little turn for satire,
And yet methinks the older that one grows
Inclines us more to laugh than scold, though laughter
Leaves us so doubly serious shortly after.

In this universe, what might merit satire elicits laughter,
but laughter reinforces the recognition of the inexplica-
ble seriousness of things, and becomes the index of a
critical self-restraint, not of unprincipled indulgence. Instead of the vices, the satirist, albeit sardonically,
"mourns." The material for satire is not impregnated with
the animus of satire; the "theme of encyclopaedic parody
[that] is endemic to satire"[16] loses its definition, leaving
us with something like satire *manqué.*

In keeping with his treatment of epic and satire, much
of what Byron does with his techniques and topics in
Don Juan tends to bring out the precariousness of our
conventions, our definitions, our complacencies. This is,
one may infer, a large part of the purpose behind his
cryptically avowed "method" (I.vii) or "way" (XIV.vii)
—an avowal which, we may observe, he made both early

[16] Frye, *Anatomy*, p. 322.

and late in the poem. He is not arrogating to himself the epithet "Sage" (xvii.ix-x), but agitating against slipshod conclusions on the grounds that we come no nearer to "truth" than acquaintance with "A something like it" (xvii.v-vi). His summaries of experience typically involve recognizing paradox or perversity: "Man's a strange animal"; "Man's a phenomenon, . . . wondrous"; "Love's a capricious power"; "There's nought, no doubt, so much the spirit calms / As rum and true religion"; "Man, being reasonable, must get drunk"; "The heart is like the sky, a part of heaven, / And changes night and day, too, like the sky"; "If [truth] could be told, / . . . How oft would vice and virtue places change"; "There is no sterner moralist than Pleasure. . . ." Even an apparently straightforward axiom, "As the soil is, so the heart of man" (iv.lv), says more about inevitability than about consistency or clarity in human nature, since the "soil" shows self-contradictory characteristics.

The poem explicitly anticipates that, between habit and hypocrisy, there will be resentment (vii.vi, xi.lxxxix) of its unsanctified standpoint, which indeed Southey in a moment of righteous rancor called "satanic."[17] But it anticipates no rebuttal. Byron makes us, however ungraciously, bear witness to and participate in the terms of *Don Juan*. He boldly convicts us of his characters' nature or experience (i.cxii, iv.iv), or of his own nesci-

[17] M. K. Joseph, in his wide-ranging discussion of *Don Juan*, suggests another source of resentment in social and political circumstances: "The years after Waterloo were bitter and reactionary; the fear of an English revolution was real and not unfounded. The hysteria of some of the denunciations of *Cain* and *Don Juan* . . . is explained, though not justified, when seen against this background. Theological speculation and social satire endangered the 'Establishment'—all the more so in the hands of a best-selling poet so conspicuously identified with his own rebellions and satanic heroes" (*Byron the Poet*, p. 294).

ence (i.clxxix, ccxiv, iv.i, xviii, vi.xvii, viii.lxxxix, ix.xvii, xi.iii, xii.xix, xl, xvi.cix, xvii.iii). The poem, nakedly defying our shibboleths in its manner of handling subject matter and form, comes eventually to defy our no less sacred self-beliefs. If not about us, it contains us, and wherever we object to it the danger is present that we object to what will have to be recognized as ourselves, without disguise.

Ultimately Byron does not scruple to put us through the actual experience of objective disorganization and incongruity. The shipwreck alone makes a veritable textbook on the fallacies of expectation; for Byron, as Ridenour comments, would "existentially . . . bring home to us the terrible human suffering that may be caused by the formula 'Heaven's will be done,' or by any attempt easily to assert an abstract order for which [one] is unable to detect much concrete evidence" (*Style*, pp. 150-151). The emphasis, perhaps, should fall less on the suffering than on the failure of formulae, on the failure of knowledge itself. It is intended as a puzzle that "the weaklier child . . . bore up long," whereas the boy who "was more robust and hardy to the view" succumbed "early" (ii.lxxxvii-lxxxviii). Have we, it becomes necessary to ask, enough of a grasp of the nature of strong and weak to use the terms reliably? What grasp do we have of experience when our definitions of it are so precarious? The puzzle of the two deaths may be taken as a medical one, as part of a wide impenetrability in the order of merely physical occurrences. But things go no less erratically when they have imparted to them the force of human direction. Though Byron assures us that "the desire of life / Prolongs it" (lxiv), the instinct of self-preservation gets betrayed by its own logic, as the food which the voyagers desperately make of one of the party brings on a grotesque madness and death; and it is death for soul as well as body, to judge by the men's blasphemy and "despairing" (lxxix). The vignette of the three men (might they be "the three . . ." who have declined Pedrillo?) done in by eating the "turtle of the hawk's-bill kind" carries the same exemplary irony, without being merely repetitious. It helps to account for errors of expectation by pinpointing errors of perception and fantasies of faith. The three, appearing to be "asleep," are in fact *dead*, and it seems a sound conclusion that this very mistake of death for sleep has proved fatal for them: their "sleeping" turtle was most likely a floating, toxic corpse (xcviii-xcix). Not only their eyes, Byron says, but their religious assumptions and reasoning have betrayed them, since they have blindly leapt to the conclusion "that in such perils, more than chance / Had sent them this for their deliverance." The kindest thing would be to think their assumption false; if it were otherwise, what inference must follow concerning the nature of something "more than chance"? But Byron himself will go no further than to see "the world" as "at the worst . . . a glorious blunder" about which one must abstain from pontificating (*DJ* xi.iii-iv).

Throughout the shipwreck, some idea of a benevolent or reliable order is kept in mind, but its actual indices are ambiguous enough. Even without speculating whether Byron means to jog our imagination when he attributes momentary "salvation" (xxviii) to "the maker, Mr. Mann" (xxix),[18] we can note that he makes Juan's sur-

---

[18] Byron's source reads: *"The pumps,* to the excellent construction of which I owe the preservation of my life, *were made by Mr. Mann of London"* (*PW*, vi, 89n). Byron contrives, by very subtle changes, to focus gratitude on Mann where the original

vival "providential" (cvii), and then also the *destruction
of ships* with whose remnants Haidee and Zoe make a
fire (cxxxii). "Providence" is at odds with itself, or rather
our knowledge supports conflicting conclusions and beliefs regarding it. Again the rainbow, symbol of the universal covenant of safety from a watery annihilation, is
allowed in the particular emergency to enhance morale
(xciii), but proves in reality merely picturesque and
evanescent:

> Now overhead, a rainbow, bursting through
> The scattering clouds, shone, spanning the dark sea,
> Resting its bright base on the quivering blue;
> And all within its arch appear'd to be
> Clearer than that without, and its wide hue
> Wax'd broad and waving, like a banner free,
> Then changed like to a bow that's bent, and then
> Forsook the dim eyes of these shipwreck'd men.
> It changed, of course . . .
>   (xci-xcii)

The editorial "of course" in the last line quietly insists on
a naturalistic flux. On the descriptive level the rainbow
is presented as "celestial" and "heavenly"; in the practical realm it operates in terms of that flux, as a "chame-

---

concentrates on the pumps: in the process, it appears to me, a
fairly straightforward recognition of his engineering gets shifted
toward a celebration of his creativity—the engineer as puisne god.
The homonymy of his name also warrants notice: Mann (man)
is the engineer or Maker. Byron had already written, in this vein,
of "the oak leviathans, whose huge ribs make / Their clay creator
the vain title take / Of lord of thee [ocean]" (*CH* iv.clxxxi). In
this light it seems a definite undervaluation to say that for the
shipwreck "Byron carries on the verse in a hearty, prosaic tone
suitable to his temporarily-assumed role of 'honest tar,'" and
"carefully preserves the matter-of-fact reality of the original"
(Joseph, p. 170).

leon" and kaleidoscope." It is as natural, and as consequential, as a "black eye in a recent scuffle." In sum, both experience and philosophy, both history and revelation fail us in the clutch. It is but little to the purpose to speak of the "elements" of Byron's universe as "means of grace" or "occasions of sin" (Ridenour, *Style*, p. 49). In a work which so skeptically denies and defies dogmatism, these become alien and archaic categories.

The sense of incertitude, the exposition of inextricable duality is furthered in *Don Juan* by repeated use of oxymoron (e.g., Society as a "wild," or life as "melancholy merriment"); by manipulations of rhyme and stanza form[19] to create shockingly plausible associations and juxtapositions which challenge the claims of things or ideas or persons to serious attention or attachment; and by the exercise of wit, as in the definition of inconstancy and of the miser where by a singular analytical twist standard values are reversed.

As an antidote to whatever trace may still exist of the misconception of Byron as a mere leering nihilist,[20] it should be useful to look more clearly at Byron's weaving of rhyme[21] and stanza, and at his exercise of wit; in both

[19] Eduard Eckhardt gives a good descriptive analysis of Byron's ways with rhyme in "Lord Byrons komische Reime" (*E St*, LXX [1936], 198-208). Truman Guy Steffan provides a complementary analysis, dealing with the evolution of Byron's rhymes and having a distinctly evaluative temper, in *Byron's Don Juan: The Making of a Masterpiece*, Austin, Texas, 1957, pp. 170-176. In the discussion following it will be seen that I make use of both.

[20] A viewpoint still best exemplified in the comment of William Blackwood, as recorded by Mrs. Oliphant in the *Annals of a Publishing House*: "It was not the grossness of blackguardism which struck me, but it was the vile, heartless, and cold-blooded way in which this fiend attempted to degrade every tender and sacred feeling of the human heart."

[21] Incidental borrowings from Butler in Byron's comic verse have been noted by E. H. Coleridge, but the full extent of the romantic poet's indebtedness to Butler and *Hudibras* remains to

a certain social and philosophical content will be discerned. The gap between politics and truth attracts attention in *Don Juan*, where Byron speaks of

> A sort of treaty or negotiation
> Between the British cabinet and Russian,
> Maintained with all the due prevarication
> With which great states such things
> are apt to push on.
> (x.xlv)

The linking by rhyme of 'negotiation' and 'prevarica-
tion' (the off-rhyme in the alternate verses need not dis-
tract us) helps to bring home the distinction between
official nomenclature and customary—due—conduct.
Again, in a comment on flirtation, Byron makes deft use
of rhyme to penetrate a specious disguise of the word;
the conduct of "your cold coquette," he remarks, "is
merely innocent flirtation, / Not quite adultery, but
adulteration" (xii.lxiii). Here the radical closeness of
adultery and adulteration gives an added piquancy to the
rhyming conjunction of flirtation and adulteration. Finally
we may look at a couplet concerning glory (perennially
anathema to Byron), in which the rhyme word does
not so much qualify as redefine, passing absolute judgment on the nature of glory in the light of the nature of
things. The meaning of the plain statement is intensi-
fied in the compass of the pertinent rhyme:

---

be shown. In praising the wit of "matchless Hudibras" Byron
speaks of his fine manipulations of octosyllabic couplets. But this
was surely not to slight other, perhaps more vital elements of his
technique. It is hard to imagine that a poet of Byron's rhyming
propensities, shown inchoately as early as in the verses "To
Edward Noel Long, Esq.," could have failed to take notes on the
patterns of rhyme whereby Butler in considerable part expressed
his wit.

But Juan was not meant to die so soon:—
We left him in the focus of such glory
As may be won by favor of the moon
Or ladies' fancies—rather transitory. . . .
    (x.ix)

It scarcely needs saying that Byron uses his rhymes consciously, and therefore tendentiously. The evidence of the revisions he made in his rhymes is eloquent enough. And we find him, even where he has no *reason* to hold that "love rules . . . the grove," prepared to see "something in" the idea owing to the power of the *rhyme* (xII.xiii). In "The Age of Bronze" he again acknowledges the self-validating force of rhyme (see st. xiii), and in *Don Juan* he explicitly avows his sense that the relation of words in rhyme may be a relation in fact: " 'Kiss' rhymes to 'bliss' in fact as well as verse" (vI.lix). Perhaps I have not been illustrating "rhymes . . . in fact," but rhymes which reveal the naked truth beneath a cloak of self-satisfied opinion. In point of fact, these are what Byron chiefly purveys, making rhyme an "instrument of meaning" (Steffan, I, 170).

Besides debunking rhyme, the somewhat less common use of an undermining couplet stands out in the Byronic octave. The two devices are in principle akin, but the difference between them is not negligible: the efficacy of the couplet relies on incongruous juxtapositions, on bathos,[22] that of the rhyme on unorthodox comparisons.

---

[22] An interesting antecedent for Byron's use of ironical bathos is found in Buckingham's *The Rehearsal*, from which Byron owns he learned the trick of crowning a series with the casually belittling phrase "and all that" (*PW*, vi, 52). In the way of ironical bathos Buckingham of course had much more to offer Byron than this one phrase. His skill, for example, in reducing the heroic theme of love to an absurdity is hardly surpassed by Byron. Prince Pretty-

Both, however, enable Byron to project an unsentimental
light of realism onto the misty, and mist-flattered crea-
tions of dishonest thought. When he advises us that
Juan's "recent wounds might help a little" in his with-
standing of the "Romagnole's" charms (IV.xcv), he is

---

man—the name itself mocks his claims as a mighty lover—reflects
on his new experience of being in love:

> How strange a captive am I grown of late!
> Shall I accuse my love, or blame my fate?
> My love, I cannot; that is too divine:
> And against Fate what mortal dares repine?
> *Enter* Clovis.
> But here she comes.
> Sure 'tis some blazing comet, is it not? [*lies down*]
> . . . .
> But I am so surprised with sleep I cannot speak the rest.
> (II.iii)

On one level, this is meant to be a ludicrous "surprise," but it
would be cheap if it were that alone. In a special way there is no
"surprise." The character, Buckingham seems to imply, is mechanically mouthing words, not expressing true passion. He is
metaphysically asleep, and so easily falls asleep physically.

A similar artistic justice—not to mention that cruel matter,
poetic justice—is involved in the ludicrous outcome of Bayes' pre-
tentious attempt to teach the actors acting. They are "dead,"
but must rise at a given note in his music. He addresses them:

> Why, gentlemen, if there by any faith in a person that's a
> Christian, I sate up two whole nights in composing this air,
> and apting it for the business: for, if you observe, there are two
> several designs in this tune; it begins swift, and ends slow. You
> talk of time, and time; you shall see me do 't. Look you now.
> Here I am dead. [*Lies down flat on his face.*] Now mark my
> note *in effaut flat.* Strike up music. Now. [*As he rises up hastily,
> he tumbles and falls down again.*] Ah, gadsookers, I have broke
> my nose.
> (II.v)

Of course it is harder to put Bayes' artistic nose out of joint, but
the reader fully appreciates the thrusts he is exposed to. Again,
Bayes reads, for the benefit of his guests, Smith and Johnson,
Lardella's love-letter composed in the character of "a humble-
bee"; they make appropriate comments. Of these, one in particular is noteworthy, as it graphically embodies Buckingham's prac-

the thinking, perhaps the skeptical man who declines to get carried away by intemperate visions of Juan's everlasting loyalty to Haidee. Juan's blood is low, not cold. In like manner, having displayed "longings sublime" and "aspirations high" in Juan before the consummation of the affair with Julia, Byron takes care to warn us: "If *you* think 't was philosophy that this did, / I can't help thinking puberty assisted" (I.xciii).

Byron's rather intellectual "wit," his ability to turn familiar opinions inside out with a deft twist of thought, may seem the most nearly arbitrary of the devices under discussion here. Its occurrence is far from common, but is conspicuous enough to warrant attention. For Byron proves remarkably adept at witty writing, as in his claim (parallel not in Chaucer's "Wife of Bath" but in certain poems by Blake or Yeats) that the *sensual* may realize the *ideal*.

.   .   .   .   That which
Men call inconstancy is nothing more
Than admiration due where Nature's rich
Profusion with young beauty covers o'er

---

tice of correcting the eccentric and overblown in the light of the normal.

Bayes. "Your bed of love from angers I will free;
But most, from love of any future bee.
And when, with pity, your heartstrings shall crack,
With empty arms I'll bear you on my back."
Smith. A pick-a-pack, a pick-a-pack.

(IV.i)

This, too, is a just deflation, and is brought off with extraordinary deftness. One pays homage to the instinct which led Buckingham to use ellipsis for directness, and repetition for emphasis. It may fairly be supposed that Byron, if he imitated Buckingham's ironical use of 'and all that,' did not fail to appreciate the more forceful examples of bathetic irony in which *The Rehearsal* abounds.

> Some favoured object; and as in the niche
> A lovely statue almost we adore,
> This sort of adoration of the real
> Is but a heightening of the *beau ideal.*
> 　　　　(II.ccxi)

Or consider his long, symphonic divagation on gold and misers (XII.iii ff.) Here is Volpone turned reflective apologist: "Why call the miser miserable? . . . the frugal life is his, / Which in a saint or cynic ever was / The theme of praise. . . . He is your only poet. . . . On him the diamond pours its brilliant blaze, / While the mild emerald's beam shades down the dies / Of other stones to soothe the miser's eyes." And so on. Now surely a degree of sheer self-bracing play, which seems inseparable from wit, is manifest here. But more is manifest as well. With the singularity of his wit, with the sleights of his analogies and imagery Byron contrives as it were to shock us into apprehending the way our "principles," supposedly so comprehensive and precise, may subsidize what they seem to reject, being only more ineffectual as they grow more comfortable.[23]

In having recourse to wit, to wicked rhymes and "fast-break" stanza patterns, Byron is not gratuitously, or even mainly out to scuttle standard values, which in the long run his kind of examination may stimulate one to prune, prop, and furnish with constant, conscious nurture. Rather he impugns, by demonstration, the overwhelming

---

[23] In terms of motive, as opposed to the effect of his transgression of our canonical reactions, it is pertinent to recall Byron's argument for "exalting the earthly," to wit, that "the true voluptuary will never abandon his mind to the grossness of reality. It is by exalting . . . the *physique* of our pleasures, by veiling these ideas, by forgetting them altogether, or, at least, never naming them hardly to one's self, that we alone can prevent them from disgusting" (*LJ*, II, 377).

power of one source of standard values, namely language. Byron takes care to remind us that such values frequently have a linguistic base, and being skeptical of the extent to which "words make rules" (xvii.iii), he brings language itself under the poem's panoramic machinery of examination. Language proves—and this is a danger which the writing in *Don Juan* ceaselessly maneuvers to acknowledge or avoid—ungainly and opinionated in front of the quick play of actuality and, worse, susceptible to paltering. The vagaries of puberty pass for philosophy (i.xciii). Murder and "glory" (vii. xxvi), "firmness" and "obstinacy" (xiv.xc) occur as tandem terms which seem far less capable of rendering an objective position than a subjective response. Debt goes by the name of wealth (vii.xlv), demolition is called restoration (xvi.lviii), the gigolo of an Empress holds a "high official station" upon which a "matron-like interpretation" can be put (ix.xlviii, lii). (Indeed, Donna Inez—and she would be the one—speaks of the itching Catherine's "maternal love" for Juan!) In these cases Byron is exposing shoddy and vicious use of language, but it is not to be assumed that he considered it rationally or empirically possible to achieve intrinsic truth of statement. As Joseph and Donald M. Hassler say, he wished to see a correspondence between words and objects or fact, but Lovell and Alvin B. Kernan and Ridenour, among many, rightly stress that his conception of fact, of experience is informed with paradox.[24] Thus his own use of language in the great satirical triad is less cate-

[24] In order, *Byron the Poet*, p. 285; "*Marino Faliero*, the Byronic Hero, and *Don Juan*." *K-SJ*, xiv (1965), 57-63; "Irony and Image in *Don Juan*," passim; *The Plot of Satire*, New Haven, 1965, pp. 182-183; and *The Style of Don Juan*, passim.

gorical than paradoxical, approximative, revising and qualifying, reflecting and amplifying.

Besides what has already been seen to this effect, it may be observed that Byron is dealing with the limitations, and not a form of vicious exploitation of language, when he writes "great names are nothing more than nominal" (iv.ci), or again "he who *names one* [love or lust], both perchance may hit on." Similarly, he dramatizes the general inadequacy of single statements by calling both Juan and Lord Henry Amundeville "all things to all men," and presenting the supposition that love is woman's whole existence in regard to both Haidee and Julia. His carefulness with language, which as a rule expresses itself not by rich phrasal intensity but by intensifying reverberation, shades into the question of the reliability of knowledge, as appears in the following quotation:

> Apologue, Fable, Poesy, and Parable,
> Are false, but may be render'd also true,
> By those who sow them in a land that's arable,
> 'T is wonderful what Fable will not do!
> 'T is said it makes Reality more bearable:
> But what's Reality? Who has its clue?
> Philosophy? No: she too much rejects.
> Religion? *Yes*; but which of all her sects?
>   (xv.lxxxix)

Byron's consciousness of literary convention, and of the power of literary convention, is undeniable; still this is far from meaning that he pursued or even advocated formal decorum in *Don Juan*. Obeying forms means denying realities, and in addition to the *impropriety* of stylistic decorum for an audience both out of step and

out of sympathy with it (the romantic preface teaches
or preaches, the neoclassical preface more confidently
apologizes and flatters), it is hard to conceive what form
or style could be proper to a poem that presumably covers "everything" in a "checkered" world.

Early in his life Byron contended that "to be . . . in
doubt" was "the *ne plus ultra* of mortal faith" (*LJ*, ɪɪ, 349).
It is a home principle of his great masterwork, the point of
origin and terminus alike of the poem's material, promul-
gated in the utterances of "more than Humean skepticism"[25] which resound antiphonally through it. It could
be argued that Byron developed, or even discovered this
focus ex post facto in the very current of composition.
His major utterances of skepticism are concentrated in,
though not confined to the middle and later cantos. In
point of fact it would seem out of place and practically
premature in, say, the first two cantos for Byron to write
as he does in the sixth:

> I love Wisdom more than she loves me;
> My tendency is to philosophize
> On most things, from a tyrant to a tree;
> But still the spouseless virgin *Knowledge* flies.
> What are we? and whence came we? what shall be
> Our *ultimate* existence? what's our present?
> Are questions answerless and incessant.

Still it would hold true that the discovery was germinat-
ing from the start, in the asystematic and as it were incidental movement of *Don Juan*, with its contradictions
and deflections, its abrupt formations and dissolutions,

[25] George M. Ridenour, "Byron in 1816: Four Poems from
Diodati," in *From Sensibility to Romanticism*, p. 454.

through which Byron is effectively dramatizing and *championing* an "uncertainty of . . . point of view."

The appropriate atmosphere has of course been made familiar in *Beppo*, wherein Byron manages to show a certain moral and intellectual insouciance or naïveté and also a steady critical, quasi-religious sense of *honestum*. Concerning the latter, which has gone undiscussed[26] largely owing to the interests of the former position, a brief statement may not come amiss.

It appears that Byron, though he deprecates "love ideal" as being, like "ideal beauty," merely a "fine name," stops short of canonizing the peculiarities of actual love. This is only fitting in one who was to write, "There is no sterner moralist than Pleasure" (*DJ* III.lxv). His capsule history of a love affair, ostensibly *dégagé*, turns out to be implicitly evaluative.

> For glances beget ogles, ogles sighs,
> Sighs wishes, wishes words, and words a letter,
> Which flies on wings, of light-heel'd Mercuries,
> Who do such things because they know no better;
> And then, God knows what mischief may arise,
> When love links two young people in one fetter,
> Vile assignations, and adulterous beds,
> Elopements, broken vows, and hearts, and heads.
> (*Beppo*, xvi)

The idea of knowing no better, and terms like "mischief," "vile," "adulterous," and "broken vows" all have a pejora-

---

[26] Ian Jack has made some penetrating, if all too brief remarks on the weighted buoyancy of *Beppo*, seeing that in it "we find satire as well as joking" and move not in a "world of fun" but in a "world of mischief" (*English Literature 1815-1832*, p. 63), and Robert F. Gleckner proposes that its laughter be seen as "merely the mask of despair," favoring "a more somber reading of the poem" (*Ruins*, pp. 302, 303).

tive ring; and it should be noted that in the final verse
the moral fact (broken vows) causes and defines the
personal and physical consequences (broken hearts and
heads). Far from adhering to an amoral chronological
order, the pattern of this lugubrious series manifests the
public disorder that spreads from a private moral fault.
A negative view, admittedly expressed more in terms of
sorrow than of wrath, comes through this description of
love's career, and again through Byron's statement that
while a special quality in Youth may *lend* love "joy, and
sweetness, vigor, truth, / Heart, soul . . . ," an accounting
comes and love, languishing, always "grows uncouth"
(lv). As Byron remarked to the Countess of Blessington,
"Liaisons that are not cemented by marriage, must produce unhappiness, when there is refinement of mind,
and that honourable 'fiérte' which accompanies it."

The sense of the uncouth which informs the portrayal
of love in *Beppo* may result from the seniority of the participants, but more than passage of time is at issue. A
definite pattern of censoriousness emerges from diction
and imagery. Byron calls it "a grievous sin" for a woman
to have a "Cavalier Servente," and holds the custom to be
tantamount "(not to say the worst)" to "A *second* marriage
which corrupts the *first*" (xxxvi). He describes the Count,
perhaps punningly, as a "*vice*-husband" (xxix). The system of "Serventismo" he dubs as "sinful doings" (xli), a
phrase which exquisitely combines a frown—sinful—and
a giggle—doings—to typify his position. And finally, he
makes an arresting suggestion as to how "Serventismo"
is perpetuated: the flesh sees to it (of this contention no
proof can be required); and the world and the devil
see to it.

> The world beheld them with indulgent air;
> The pious only wish'd "the devil take them!"
> He took them not; he very often waits,
> And leaves old sinners to be young ones' baits.
> (liv)

The Vision of Judgment will remind us that hell, to get peopled, can do nothing better than to leave people "to themselves" (st. xli).

The imagery Byron employs in painting the gondola, the vessel of love, likewise suggests an attitude less than licentious. He dwells on terms that call to mind the idea of death, not so much with literal implications as with the purpose of bringing out the incongruity, even the indecency, of such conduct in such circumstances. The explicit identification of the gondola with a "mourning couch" can only half surprise us, since it brings into the center of focus an idea vibrating on the periphery for some time before. The gondola, Byron tells us,

> glides along the water looking *blackly*.
> Just like a *coffin* clapt in a canoe,
> Where none can make out what you say or do.

> And up and down the long canals they go,
> And under the Rialto shoot along,
> By night and day, all paces, swift or slow,
> And round the theatres, a *sable* throng.
> They wait in their *dusk livery of woe*,—
> *But not to them do mournful things belong*,
> For sometimes they *contain a deal of fun*,
> *Like mourning coaches when the funeral's done*.
> (xix-xx; italics added throughout)

Indulgent laughter is audible throughout *Beppo*, but it has a continual undertone of sardonic morality. We should not mistake the narrator's French, or rather Italian factualness for mere naïveté—he is a man who combines knowledge and resignation, who has his principles and perceptions, but without a temptation to canonize them as assertions and pronouncements. It has been argued that "the poem's success depends on the exclusion of the poet's profounder moral attitudes and deepest beliefs about mankind and society" (Rutherford, p. 122). But these are always obliquely present, reflecting critical shadows on the merry surface of the tale, and making the poem's success more substantial and complex than at first appears. The narrator, who sounds genuinely appreciative when he speaks of "a deal of fun," contrives to make us aware of his principles without making an issue of them. He renders, and even implicitly judges reality, but declines to quarrel with it.

If *Beppo* makes a less consummate rehearsal and miniature of *Don Juan* than "Tintern Abbey" of *The Prelude*, it is in the main because *Beppo* leaves implicit or inert the force of analysis that surges everywhere in *Don Juan*, set free perhaps in the first instance by the story, but ultimately deflecting, if not directing any given passage of the narrative. For *Don Juan* forms an investigation, as comprehensive and immethodical as Byron's complex life and wide-flung reading, of the content of experience and history and opinion. It embodies the process of turning "back regards / On what I've seen or ponder'd" (xiv.xi). The poem has no action in the Aristotelian sense; with only a beginning ("preludios") after sixteen odd cantos it seeks to claim none. In terms of Coleridge's categorical statement that "the common end of all *narrative* . . . Poems is to convert a *series* into a *Whole*,"[27]

[27] *Collected Letters*, ed. Earl Leslie Griggs, Oxford, 1956-59, IV, 545.

it would seem to have gone astray as narrative; but again with roughly one third of its substance put to other than narrative uses, according to figures compiled by Joseph (*Byron the Poet*, p. 334), and with its obvious sense that existence is not integral, but serial, it sets up no pretense to typological decorum. It is instead of a type, an example of poetry, according to the most temperate and poignant definition Byron put forth: "A paper kite which flies 'twixt life and death, / A shadow which the onward soul behind throws" (xiv.viii). Poetry, it would seem, involves recollection, or rather reflection, and it is for the purpose of reflection that Byron so persistently, as Joseph says, "distances" us from the narrative (*Byron the Poet*, passim). What Eliot describes as a "genius for divagation"[28] in Byron was at once a richer and a more deliberate technique than that critic seemed to know.

Byron nevertheless recognizes the unconventional character of the poem, and he essentially describes it, first as a case of "now and then narrating, / Now pondering" (ix.lii), and then even more plainly:

> This narrative is not meant for narration,[29]
> But a mere airy and fantastic basis,
> To build up common things with common places.
> (xiv.vii)

Common things here do not amount to any philosophical affirmation; as Byron says, "philosophy . . . too much rejects," and besides he has sympathetically but distinctly led up to his comment on common things with an avowal

---

[28] "Byron," in *From Anne to Victoria: Essays by various hands*, ed. Bonamy Dobrée, New York, 1937, p. 605.

[29] Joseph takes it for granted that Byron is being nothing but preciously paradoxical and facetious with this statement (*Byron the Poet*, p. 198). The line has its funny qualities, to be sure, but they also contain a bright, solid kernel of truth.

of enforced agnosticism. Byron is building up an edifice of examination and analysis, ranging from the raw material of description and episode, in which, as Elizabeth Boyd observes, his "ideas are implicit" (*Byron's Don Juan*, p. 59), through the middle ground of critical reflection, to the distant pole of general speculation. The structure of analysis is unmistakable where Byron sets out the hierarchy of love before the Catherine episode (ix.lxxiii-lxxvi), its contribution to the poem's skepticism arising of course from the uncertain use of the categories: Juan is apotheosized in his most materialistic affair, with the Empress, and ultimately becomes an inferior material reflector in the affair with the luminous Haidee. It is nothing but praeteritio for Byron to come in with: "Well, we won't analyse" (lxxvii). The story does often "tell for itself" (*ibid.*), but it gains its characteristic range and resonance from continuing analysis.

More oblique uses of analysis also need to be recognized. Let us take a viable phase of the Juan-Julia episode, getting underway with the fatal *moonshine* and rounded off at the no less portentous *cloudy night* (i.cxiii-cxxxv, 1).[30] The contrasting frame so obviously signals contrasting moods and actions that attention is to some extent diverted from its value as a signal of time. But Byron seems to desire definite attention to the passage of time. He sharpens our awareness with the blatant artifice of stanzas cxx-cxxi, where some supposedly

[30] Much the same passage is taken up by Joseph, who, however, accepts at face value the broad range of materials Byron brings up. His analysis is predominantly sequential and cursory, with little sense of the coherent forward thrust I have tried to show in the passage. This kind of relation will again obtain in our several discussions of Lambro's homecoming.

wicked license turns out to be chronological merely;[31] and he dapples the verse with various time-connected references, to Xerxes and Plato and Adam and Prometheus, to anniversary resolutions, to sociological and technological history, to the uncertainty of the future. The seemingly casual time frame of the excerpt thus acquires considerable depth and reticularity. We are seeing Juan and Julia through a telescope of time, and we are asked to analyze and understand their actions in that focus. It is not a disability but an inevitability that, at a generous count, no more than 33 of the 177 lines in question represent direct narrative.

The relationship of Juan and Julia is made to appear singular, yet typical, and fresh, while also ageless. Initially Byron counterpoints the narration (cxiii.1, cxv, cxvii) with careful definition of external factors that prime the erotic moment by overcoming (the moon, cxiii.2-cxiv) or by undermining (Platonic philosophy, cxvi) possible resistance. The moon and Plato (the material and the mental?) further have in common a certain duplicity; the reputedly chaste and modest-looking moon fosters mischief and "business in a wicked way," while Plato's system is seen as fantasy, fancy, feigning, and charlatanry. Byron here turns to the inner motivation of the moony, platonizing pair, to wit Pleasure, and shows us its antiquity and unoriginality (cxviii) and imperviousness to the thought of consequences (cxix), and

---

[31] A sidelight of this passage is its betrayal of the reader into a conspiracy of indecent indignation with Byron. The pursed lip which greets his warning that his "chaste Muse a liberty must take" will surely, when the liberty is found to be merely literary, slacken into a sheepish grin. What, after all, have been our expectations? And if we are willing to make chaste mean unchaste, as regards Byron's muse, do we abide by that decision on finding we are "chaster" yet?

THE BLIND MAN TRACES THE CIRCLE

then its varieties, which can be classified as aesthetic (cxxii), domestic (cxxiii), social, subdivided into urban and rural, and further subdivided into pleasures of special groups (cxxiv), and finally individual and miscellaneous (cxxv-cxxvi). This section culminates with, makes a foil for the pleasure being shared by Juan and Julia—oddly enough, though this is ostensibly the pleasure of love, it seems to be intrinsically the pleasure of novelty, whose contradictions and perversities are ominously illustrated as a note of dubiety ("Man is strange . . . wondrous") breaks in upon the axiomatic certainty ("Sweet is . . .") of the litany of pleasures. The tumultuous bedroom scene will richly justify the contention that "Few mortals know what end they would be at," just as Juan and Julia's approach to this point has anticipated it. But Byron is aiming beyond a moral summary of their affair. By placing the logic of analysis before the logic of narration, Byron elicits from a mere encounter in love, by means of an extraordinary range of reference, a major statement of man's unpromising adventures against time and his unavailing presumption of knowledge. Perhaps it would be proper to acknowledge an alternative frame for the excerpt, starting with the inability to resist the rising moon and ending with the impossibility of resisting the setting sun: "sober suns *must* set" (italics added). Obviously from the standpoint of a plot with a beginning, middle, and end, little applause is forthcoming for the passage; its logic, its value must be recognized elsewhere, in the invariable mortality of human things and acts, in the weltering system of change.

An oblique and suggestive organization also marks the long passage on Lambro's homecoming, up to the confrontation with Haidee (III.xx-IV.xxxv). The passage breaks down into two main parts. The first is predominantly spatial, and follows Lambro's progress from his ship to his hall, with a simultaneous presentation of the whole social scheme, from children playing, to girls dancing, to "old smokers" sedately listening to fantastic stories; from the idleness and festivity of domestics to that of the mistress and new "master." The inclusivity of it all is suggested by the narrator's lists of "song, dance, wine, music, stories," and of "rice, meat, dancing, wine, and fiddling." The culminating scene of "the lady and her lover . . . / At wassail in their beauty and their pride" has its own appropriate architecture, too, as the eye (Lambro's?) after fixing them (lxi.1-4) sweeps over the large scene (lxi.5-lxiii) then moves up (lxiv-lxv) and then downward again to Juan and Haidee (lxvii) as a starting point for a new, more rapid spotting of the hall's accoutrements which will again culminate with Haidee and Juan (lxx-lxxvii), before the festivity seen outside is brought within, by the "suite" of "Dwarfs, dancing girls, black eunuchs, and a poet" (lxxviii).

This spatial phase, though not devoid of references to long-gone times and places (xxiii, lxxiv), is chiefly concerned with establishing the present state and immediate possibilities of the narrative. Even so, one could see in it an illustration, on an elementary level, of an analytical impulse to recognize the multifariousness of individual scenes. A more philosophical analysis in this case follows, rather than being interspersed with the narrative proper, as Byron uses Haidee's time-serving poet (lxxx) to initiate the theme of time which will, after expanding and complicating the context in which the lovers are judged, swing in upon them again, and their imminent disaster. (In particular this poet, a singer of time [lxxix] and yet a truckler to circumstances, may be said to prepare for Byron's remarks on Wordsworth—for it is more than the combination of leisure and pique that finds Wordsworth a place here—within the analysis of the ways of time; he also reminds us of Southey, whose changeableness Byron may resent less than his self-ignorance and dishonesty.)

In the temporal phase of the passage, which is *mutatis mutandis* no less conspicuously marked than the spatial (we can reckon reminders of time by the tens from III. lxxix to IV.xxxv), Byron develops two complementary perspectives. The first is a primarily conceptual sense of time as bearer of a pandemic degeneration; "these times" fall much below the past (III.lxxxvii, xciv, c), though Byron is careful to remind us that *it* was confessedly imperfect (xci-xcii, xcviii)—as he says in "The Age of Bronze," "all times when old are good." The second is a primarily emotional response to time as exterminator of everything dear ("Ah! surely nothing dies but something mourns," cviii). From either perspective the relationship of Juan and Haidee appears in an ominous light; we see the dual menace of time as the essential, while the intruding Lambro will be the effective enemy of their splendid physical sanctuary. But the ominous light also is made to serve as a foil for their relationship. Before the confrontation with Lambro, before we get to see the depth of Haidee's consciousness in love, that relationship appears rather entranced than spiritually profound; Zoe both saves and detracts from the love affair by remembering to get up some eggs. And yet in itself the love relationship has distinct overtones of the primitive in its very sanctuary, the cave; and overtones of the animal in the vital moment of mouth-to-mouth resuscitation where Haidee is "prying into his [mouth] for breath";[32] and overtones of the stealthy and the naughty in the "precautions" whereby Haidee keeps Juan "unknown," a gesture which prolongs their love but keeps Juan a delicious chattel, a pet bird or an "ocean-treasure." We too readily treat the love of Juan and Haidee as though it purely *is*, and then gets destroyed; there is more to it than the "magic, time-annihilating bubble of young love approached, menaced, and finally punctured by the slow-moving arrow of retribution" (Blackstone, pp. 207-208). Actually it grows, on Haidee's part at least, from touching and winsome, in the syndrome of fasting and hiding and warbling intercourse, to great, in the open opposition to Lambro. The cave protects and also confines, the hall threatens but also defines the pair in love. The full amplitude and power of the love they share emerges because they emerge from the cave, and so tacitly, irreversibly commit themselves to living out, rather than parcelling up that love (does Juan, who seems content to stay indefinitely in Julia's bedclothes, perhaps chafe at being housed indefinitely in the cave?). We discover the transcendent nature of possible love outside of the cave, from Haidee's refusal to retreat before Lambro into the obeying, anxious young girl she had been, and surrender the independent woman she had become. Time and the world mean more to her greatness

---

[32] Blackstone sees in this moment "a vampire note" and speaks of Haidee as "intensely predatory" (*The Lost Travellers*, p. 201); this judgment seems too harsh in tone, too much in harmony with the more obviously false note of taking Haidee as an example of super-concupiscent womankind instinctively recognized by the barely conscious Juan, who with the no less punctual instinct of self-preservation straightway "sinks back into unconsciousness!" (*ibid.*).

than the static "Edenic" retreat. Only in the world and in time does her adolescent, if appealing, relationship with Juan become richly mature and exemplary.

In a degenerate world, it is pristine; in a world of material death, it reacts on the imagination as materially uncontaminated, and emerges thereby with an imaginative immortality (iv.vii ff.). Thus when death is fastening its final grip on Haidee (to a certain extent Juan has been subordinated by the fact that Haidee is the deliberate, he the adventitious partner in the act of sacrifice, and by the ultimate statement that Haidee was "Too pure even for the purest human ties" (iii.lxxiv), Byron can with a slight shift in imagery conclusively reaffirm her immortal, her divine condition of being:

> The ruling passion, such as marble shows
> When exquisitely chisell'd, still lay there,
> But fix'd as marble's unchanged aspect throws
> O'er the fair Venus, but for ever fair. . . .
> (iv.lxi)

Haidee has become her own imaginative and spiritual permanence, with "energy like life," and yet "not life," since she is "still the same" (*ibid.*). Some comparison with the "Ode on a Grecian Urn" seems a piquant possibility; indeed Byron, in his ampler way, gives us a picture of the "little town" forsaken for a sacrifice to time (lxxii).

The departure from the strict narrative movement may have troubled Bryon, as though perhaps he lacked the full courage of his innovation (see iii.xcvi, ci, cx, iv.vii); but what he sacrifices in economy and intensity of impact he seems to make up for in a massive, slow momentum. It is doubtless in this way that Byron makes it difficult to "separate commentary from 'digression' properly so-called" (Joseph, p. 199). For he is not deviating from a settled narrative contract, but using overtly narrative passages within a total analytical complex whose method is ad lib instead of conventional, and so allowing himself a free selection from the utmost perimeter of relevance. Yet this liberty has its own rectitude, and almost seems to save itself from the danger of aimlessness and dissipation:

> Ah! what should follow slips from my reflection;
> Whatever follows ne'ertheless may be
> As a-propos of hope or retrospection
> As though the lurking thought had follow'd free.
>   (xv.i)

Interestingly enough, in this connection, the snake-like accretion which seems to mar and detract from *The Giaour* as a single narrative[33] becomes a salient and useful indication of the ultimate tendency of Byron's style. Byron is evidently feeling or blindly expanding his way in *The Giaour* toward a more than narrative statement. One is struck with the elaborate descriptions for the sake of what proves a fairly static atmosphere or setting, as in the passages on the Giaour on horseback, on Leila, on Hassan's hall; struck with the protracted and retarding relation of battles, as between the Giaour's and Hassan's bands, and of tangential scenes, like that of Hassan's mother vainly expecting him home. A moralizing and psychologizing strain is also awkwardly noticeable, viz. in the passage that begins: "The Mind, that broods o'er guilty woes. . . ." And Byron seems to let himself, in the

[33] See William H. Marshall, "The Accretive Structure of Byron's *The Giaour*," *MLN*, lxxvi (1961), 502-509.

treatment of the qualities of Beauty and Love, and in the passage beginning, "If solitude succeed to grief," indulge in stilted philosophizing. Conventionally seen as malformations in the narrative frame, such features do of course show how much Byron had yet to learn in 1813; only hindsight can say what exactly he was to learn, namely how to encompass similar features as coequal with the narrative line in a reformed analytical approach to narration: the kind of approach which makes the description of battle in *Don Juan* so much more substantial, if less relentlessly graphic, than the battle scene in "The Siege of Corinth."

The hypothesis of an analytical style, in conjunction with the agnostic philosophy that is salient in *Don Juan*, will make more tractable the Briarean compass of the work. If we must dogmatically adhere to the definition of "aesthetic experience" as "experience of a rapt, intransitive attention on an object that, because of its organization, captures and retains attention upon itself,"[34] then *Don Juan* is too angular, too insistent on self-consciousness and self-doubt in the reader to afford an aesthetic experience. On this principle, as Donald Davie protests in *Purity of Diction in English Verse*, "the poem as artifact has utterly disappeared" (p. 131). But it is tempting to see *Don Juan* the way Lovell has insisted it should be seen, as a *pertinent* artifact; and its pertinence resides in its being a sort of contest with the "omnipotence" of "opinion," with Byron deliberately reaching out in all directions for matter that must be included according to the terms of his announced theme, "things existent,"

[34] Eliseo Vivas, "Philosophy of Culture, Aesthetics, Criticism: Some Problems," *The Texas Quarterly*, ix (Spring 1966), p. 234.

or "human things and acts."[35] And if the multifariousness of "human things" seems to "defy the poet's powers of reconciliation" (Lovell, *Record*, p. 237), it bears remembering that the lack of reconciliation is in part visited upon the poet, in part tendentiously created by him as answerable to the permanent order of human being. Nor does this in any way involve him in the imitative fallacy—he is creating the recognition of disorder where it has been blinked or denied, and exploring the terms of a truer fidelity to the demands and interdictions of our knowledge, our judgments, our aspirations. In dealing with the "phenomenon" man on the basis of a fluid series rather than of a plotted coherence, Byron almost appears to have anticipated a principle not long ago formulated by the anthropologist Loren Eisley: "Man is not really visible or definable. He must be encountered."

Still, there are critical ways in which Byron swerves from the rigorous norm of encounter. His is not the uncanny attitude of a Wallace Stevens, in *Notes Toward a Supreme Fiction*, riding on an agile and genial expectancy and acceptance of the world in progress, ever developing, never defined. The difference has a twofold origin, in the more ignitable subject matter of Byron's work, and in the more ignitable responses of Byron himself. In Harold Bloom's words, "Byron despaired of apocalypse, and yet could not be content with Man or Nature as given" (*The Visionary Company*, p. 287). Thus a residue of hope, a modicum of pain are betrayed in his statement of "what we are."

[35] A strange but impressive resonance develops in this phrase when set beside the following lines from *Childe Harold* IV: "From mighty wrongs to petty perfidy, / Have I not seen what *human things* could do?" (cxxxvi; italics added).

Oftentimes, when Pegasus seems winning
The race, he sprains a wing, and down we tend,
Like Lucifer when hurled from Heaven for sinning;
Our sin the same, and hard as his to mend,
Being Pride, which leads the mind to soar too far,
Till our weakness shows us what we are.
　　　(*DJ* iv.i)

On one level Byron, the potential satirist, is signalizing the empirical void between man's performance and his professions, but on another level, almost the apostate satirist, he identifies himself with us in weakness and confesses the metaphysical void between man's conceptions and his capacities. Thus he ends up poised between a sharp recognition of things in their imperfection and a sardonic resignation to things as they are.

The fact that such a position may constitute a counterweight to an extravagant romantic optimism—the philosophy of a mental Phaëthon[36] the morning after—could partially vindicate its negative bearing, for it can suffice, to safeguard us against the Mephistophelean extreme of romantic irony and skepticism, that we assert too little out of fear of asserting too much. Byron only too clearly apprehended the lesson prepared for Arnold in *The Deformed Transformed*, that the purest conceivable beauty or glory will cast the shadow of a monster. Yet a real negative bias remains in this philosophy of abstention. The issue that takes shape, then, is whether an extremely "rebated" satire, to use Dryden's term, or solipsistic herosim, or both together, will adequately represent Byron's mind.

[36] An allusion to Phaëthon may be latent in the mention of "Pride, which leads the mind to soar too far." A certain running together of poetry and Phaëthon has appeared already in *The Vision of Judgment*, where the bard "fell like Phaëthon" (civ).

THE LIMITS OF SKEPTICISM:
THE BYRONIC AFFIRMATION

As skepticism becomes both complete
and profound, we face either a true civilization
or a blank. WALLACE STEVENS

It becomes a question, and indeed a vexed question, whether we can find in Byron's verse some affirmative philosophic position, befitting a poet of his rank and of his years. Keats died a full ten years younger than Byron, and yet left a declaration of engagement upon a philosophy which he constantly wrestled with in letters and poetry, so that some critics, though enamored of his accomplishment, regard it as but the shadow of a magnitude. By contrast, Byron may seem to boggle at the several questions that a philosophy will encompass.

The undeniable sagacity and polish of his mature satires do not cover up their disheartened skepticism: "Pray tell me, can you make fast, / After due search, your faith to any question?" (*DJ* xiv.ii). Rather they reinforce it. Byron, the romantic ironist, continually entices us with the apple of vision, only at the peak of aspiration or faith to spin into prominence the dismaying worm of "reality." He is at pains to convince us that his failure of faith results inevitably from the nature of experience, and equally determined to keep us mindful of a tradition of skepticism that buttresses his position. He calls upon figures like Socrates, Pyrrho, Hume and Montaigne to testify that "nothing can be known." And he tells us in his own right that to be "in doubt is the *ne plus ultra* of mortal faith." Skepticism thus takes on the appearance of an absolute and all-encompassing philosophy.

In actuality, few philosophical skeptics have failed in one way or another to transcend the paralysis such a position implies, to come to terms with the "vital compulsion to posit and believe something, even in the act of doubting."[1] Certainly neither Socrates, nor Pyrrho, nor Hume, nor Montaigne really upholds Byron's extremism. It is tendentious in him to put Socrates down as a skeptic. The great adversary of absolute skepticism or *sophistry*, Socrates made the condition of knowing that he knew nothing the sure first step toward sound and true knowledge. Similarly Pyrrho, far from drifting in "a sea of speculation," found at once a rudder and a harbor in dedication to serenity of mind and superiority to outward phenomena. Where Hume is concerned it should do merely to recall his footnote to the final chapter of *Dialogues concerning Natural Religion*:

> No philosophical dogmatist denies that there are difficulties both with regard to the senses and to all science; and that these difficulties are in a regular, logical method, absolutely insolvable. No sceptic denies that we lie under an absolute necessity, notwithstanding these difficulties, of thinking, believing, and reasoning with regard to all kinds of subjects, and even of frequently assenting with confidence and security.

In Montaigne, the writer whose works he made sure

---

[1] George Santayana, *Scepticism and Animal Faith; Introduction to a System of Philosophy*, New York, 1923, p. 15. See also Franklin L. Baumer, *Religion and the Rise of Scepticism*, New York, 1960, pp. 31-34, for a fuller presentation of this idea.

of taking among a mere handful of books on his great political, action-bound voyage to Greece, Byron may appear to have discovered something close to an ultimate skeptic; as R. L. Colie writes in "The Rhetoric of Transcendence," Montaigne "could never fully acquiesce either in the idea of a right reason common to all mankind or in the idea of a universal law of nature. His *Apologie* is the classic Renaissance statement of the dilemmas of knowledge, with all their intricate interrelatedness."[2] I submit, though, that if Byron does not misrepresent the fact of Montaigne's position, he misrepresents its spirit, and its effects. For Montaigne is more gracious and generous, more serene than Byron makes out; or is. According to Paul Stapfer in his *Montaigne,* the model skeptic of the Renaissance "envisage sans horreur, d'un coeur ferme et serein, même avec une gaieté qui n'est que le sourire de la bonne santé et du calme, l'impuissance de la raison humaine."[3] And it is worth repeating, to offset the defeatist undertones of the motto we make one with the name of Montaigne, Stapfer's judgment that "Distinguo, ou . . . *j'examine, je discerne*, aurait pu être la devise de Montaigne tout aussi justement que le fameux *Que sais-je?*" (*ibid.,* p. 71). It will be of some interest that *j'examine* and *je discerne* both accurately render the Greek word *skeptomai* from which "skeptic" is derived.

In short, skepticism is not historically a dead end, but a difficulty for and at times an instrument of affirmation. It would seem otherwise with Byron. How genuinely inquisitive or purposive is his skepticism? In the mature satires one exists in a world of such fluid perspective

[2] PQ, XLIII (1964), 153.
[3] (Paris, 1895), p. 91.

and mutable value that George III slips into heaven,[4] Beppo is put in the wrong (his appearance, unlike Laura's behavior, is unusual, and so unacceptable), and Lambro is at once *simpático* as a disenchanted man "stung . . . from a slave to an enslaver," and disagreeable as the rough disenchanter of Juan and Haidee. One can almost hear Byron's shrugging but inflexible comment: "Such things are."

Conversely, Byron's dramas and tales typically present heroes of "fixt mind" and "unconquerable Will," having all the solipsistic, soaring defiance of Satan with little of the power that makes him notable (how odd a figure Satan cuts, away from the scene of his power, "at home" with Sin and Death). Attempts to repeal society or cancel nature in the tales and dramas appear to rest on the assumption that it would be impossible to ameliorate either.

A certain incapacity to come to terms with the reali-

[4] The rather fluid principles of the poem are obliquely reinforced in its final line, which has the king "practising the hundredth psalm." The culminating line of the Psalm seems especially germane to *The Vision*: "For the Lord is good; his mercy is everlasting; and his truth endureth to all generations." This moral is demonstrated with more humor than invincible precision in the poem's action, where mercy seems fortuitous enough, and truth, to mortal reason at least, deeply obscure. Herein lies not only a perfect cap to the entire commentary on Southey's crude and presumptuous rigor in his *A Vision of Judgment*, but also a typical statement of the older Byron's deliberately unsettling attitude. Not that he passed beyond acerbity: the Dedication of *Don Juan*, particularly when it focuses on politics, says otherwise. But his acerbity is defensive and non-dogmatic, or anti-dogmatic. The following lines from *The Island*, coincidentally dealing with the eternal disposition of the human soul, clearly reflect his special alliance of indignation and hesitation: "Who doom to hell, themselves are on the way, / Unless these bullies of eternal pains / Are pardon'd their bad hearts for their worse brains" (iv.xii).

ties of existence manifests itself, then, in the peculiarly Byronic satires as well as in the "heroic"[5] plays and tales. Byron appears unable to negotiate the gap, which so haunted his consciousness, between our conceptions and aspirations and our capacities.

Even in his much-praised spirit of republicanism and belief in freedom[6] one should recognize at least a measure of ambivalence. Byron plainly states in *Don Juan* that he would say "fie on" revolution, but that insufferable rulers seemed to force people to it by way of despair (VIII.1-li). There are even grounds for believing that Byron, while he spoke of revolution as inevitable, held virtuous constitutional monarchy to be an ideal. Such an attitude is patent in *Don Juan*:

> He saw, however, at the closing session
>> [of Parliament],
> That noble sight, when *really* free the nation,
> A King in constitutional possession
> Of such a Throne as is the proudest station,
> Though Despots know it not—till the progression
> Of Freedom shall complete their education.
> 'T is not mere splendour makes the show august
> To eye or heart—it is the People's trust.

It is also the burden of the remarkable "Sonnet to George the Fourth," in which, while invoking his usual distinction between "despotism" and "true kingship" (True-blood, *The Flowering of Byron's Genius*, p. 153), he re-

---

[5] Fuller discussion of the heroic cast of such plays as *Marino Faliero* and *Sardanapalus* is available in my article on "The Restoration Ethos of Byron's Classical Plays" (*PMLA*, LXXIX [1964]), 569-578.

[6] The case for Byron as a political liberal is argued by András Horn in *Byron's "Don Juan" and the Eighteenth-Century English Novel*, pp. 17-27.

defines despotism rather than offering republicanism as a good; the ideal world of the poem is one of paradox, but there is no mistaking its monarchical bias:

> To be the father of the fatherless,
> To stretch the hand from the throne's height,
>   and raise
> *His* offspring, who expired in other days
> To make thy sire's sway by a kingdom less,—
> *This* is to be a monarch, and repress
> Envy into unutterable praise.
> Dismiss thy guard, and trust thee to such
>   traits,
> For who would lift a hand, except to bless?
> Were it not easy, sir, and is't not sweet
> To make thyself beloved? and to be
> Omnipotent by mercy's means? for thus
> Thy sovereignty would grow but more
>   complete:
> A despot thou, and yet thy people free,
> And by the heart, not hand, enslaving us.

Having reservations about Byron's commitment to republicanism, we seem to be left with the conclusion that he stands as a major poet affirming nothing. A recent critic is unequivocal about this.

> Byron was a figure set apart from any direct participation in a tradition of belief or developing intellectual position. . . . He was unable to find and accept an intellectual basis for existence as an absolutist, and at the same time he appears to have been emotionally incapable of subscribing to relativism as a position for an essentially posi-

tive view of existence. His being seems to reflect a fundamental split between skepticism and the impulse to believe and belong.[7]

All this is true enough of Byron (and of Coleridge and Shelley too, for what has come to seem the modern dilemma in philosophy began as a romantic problem). But it is less conclusive than it may sound. The options emerging from Byron's work do not seem to be exhausted by rationalism and religion, nor do they seem to have been uniformly hopeless. Byron's skepticism has its limits too, and not merely in terms of his being "awed by his own audacity" and refusing to face directly the full implications of his thought (Bostetter, p. 283). Something more affirmative appears in his work at least as early as *Lara* (II.x); and, occurring later in the very heart of his idio-satirical and heroic works, contrasts with and potentially redefines their dominant temper. This is a third, viable option in Byron's thought, the peculiar form of humanism and stoicism that may be called counter-heroic. It rebukes the desperate activity of the heroic no less than the desperate passivity of the idio-satirical, by virtue of

[7] Marshall, *The Structure*, p. 15. George Rebec basically advances the same idea, but in terms of praise, when he calls Byron "the greatest poet of the negative the world has seen" ("Byron and Morals," *International Journal of Ethics*, xiv [1904], 51). A remarkable blend of recognition and regret emerges in John Morley's essay on "Byron" in the *Fortnightly Review*: "There is no better proof of the enormous force of Byron's genius, than that it was able to produce so fine an expression of elements so intrinsically unfavourable to high poetry as doubt, denial, antagonism, and weariness" (viii, N. S. [1870], 652). M. K. Joseph, while appearing to believe that Byron subscribes to a positive philosophy, actually claims little more than Morley or Rebec; "Byron," he states, "stops short at the point where it is still possible to assert a . . . common human feeling, even, at times, by describing the effects of [its] absence" (*Byron the Poet*, p. 209). As if depiction of the desert meant endorsement of the garden.

its austere sense of responsibility to be principled and humane in action, to acknowledge without collapse the normal perplexities and corruptions of existence, to profit and be honored by the opportunity of confronting the self and the universe through suffering. Significantly it does not arise to meet ordinary threats to the perennial values of society, threats such as mercenariness, hypocrisy, folly, cruelty, and ambitious envy. These failings, identified as such and referred to confessed standards of conduct and belief, become objects of ridicule and scorn. But what are the confessed standards of the idiosatirical or of heroicism? Counter-heroic humanism opposes a state of emotion or passion which has been unnaturally enlarged and which therefore attains power, a virtual authority, usurping or redefining the area of value. It veritably recreates, and does not in the manner of conventional satire restore (as a painting) the terms of value. Its typical bête noire, then, would be Glory, or war, or any form of political egotism. And a typical though not necessary instrument for it would be satire.

Counter-heroic values are developed by Byron most cogently in *The Two Foscari* and in the cantos on the Siege of Ismail in *Don Juan*, where we find purified in the crucible of incandescent practicalities the mettle of acceptance and selflessness tentatively conceived in *Childe Harold* IV. *The Two Foscari* looks like the other two regular dramas in a multiplicity of ways: in the inflexibility of purpose of the chief characters, in the (imperfect) stoicism of the heroine, in its expression of demophobic feeling, its use of sophistical argumentation (by Loredano), its somewhat unsteady basis in history, and in the implicit conflict that it generates between authority and individual will. But though it may start with the same freight as *Sardanapalus* and *Marino Faliero*, it runs a decidedly different course. It is a story not of heroic action, but of heroic passion, a study of preternatural *principled* endurance of physical as well as emotional and moral torture. "What I seek to show in *The Foscaris*," Byron informed John Murray, "is the *suppressed* passion" (*LJ*, v. 372). Only in Marina is there any substantial show of a will to action. And hers is but a woman's impotent will, or perhaps rather a woman's unstable temper. She appears finally as a Laconian dame in her conviction that none but "a fearful pang" could have "wrung a groan from" her husband on the rack, and in rebuking him for his momentary despair at the prospect of banishment: "Until now thou wert / A Sufferer, but not a loud one."

So thoroughly is the heroic impulse of *Sardanapalus* reversed in *The Two Foscari* that the Doge, the protagonist, becomes the embodiment of selfless continence. Marina significantly dubs him "the stoic of the state," and if ancient Rome is invoked, as in *Marino Faliero*, it is invoked only as a model of stoicism; the Doge Foscari carries out his duties with "more than Roman fortitude." His sense of duty is presented as virtually religious:

> I have observed with veneration, like
> A priest's for the high altar, even unto
> The sacrifice of my own blood and quiet,
> Safety, and all save honour, the decrees,
> The health, the pride, the welfare of the state.

His devotion, however, demands an unremitting effort. When Marina, discovering that he is inwardly tortured by the claims of duty, asks if he is really to be pitied, she readily touches the private being in the public servant. The man in the Doge flashes forth in a brief assertion, and we feel in him the shudder that will betray the disposition to action in passionate natures passionately kept in check. He repudiates the very idea of pity, "that base word, with which men / Cloak their soul's hoarded triumph." In spurning those who would lord it over him under the disguise of pity, with what Ruskin calls "wanton tears round the humiliation of strength," Foscari creates for himself an awful loneliness. But he also displays a discrimination and a resolution equal to that state.

Clearly his is no unimaginative or footling sense of duty. He is cruelly cut by having not only to refrain from trying to succor his best-loved and last-surviving son,[8] but also to sit in inevitable judgment upon him. He is far from dissolving his sense of indignity in his sense of duty. His conduct looks rational, i.e., unemotional. But his reason strikes one as that which, as Santayana has brilliantly observed, springs from the "passion for consistency and order." He endures as he does to preserve "the welfare of the state" which would be imperiled if he were, in his own words, "disposed to brawl." He becomes thus the greatest, if not the sole bulwark of the State, and in the terms of the play superior to those whose actions he must decline to revolt against and punish. Foscari, though undergoing and not undertaking in the manner of the heroic protagonist, matches the

[8] The Tartar Khan in the Siege of Ismail (below, pp. 193 ff.) is also put to an extreme test in a context involving the life of his last-surviving and best-loved son. Unlike the Doge, he positively fights; but the difference lies between the two situations, not between the two men. In war the Tartar Khan fights, in peace the Doge suffers, both however in the only eligible way to preserve the best values of life.

latter in strength of will. But his will is differently exercised.

In the course of the drama his powers of military conquest are often referred to. What we find emphasized, though, is his power of reflection. He holds a saddened view of the human condition; what he has seen of the untrustworthiness of action has taught him the necessity of passion. What man—King Lear's "unaccommodated man"—has somehow developed to ward off the chaos of nature should be conserved at all cost. Change, even if it could be instituted as conceived, might still be undesirable, for "All things are" mysteries "to mortals":

> who can read them
> Save he who made? or, if they can, the few
> And gifted spirits, who have studied long
> That loathsome volume—man, and pored upon
> Those black and bloody leaves, his heart and brain,
> But learn a magic which recoils upon
> The adept who pursues it. . . .
> .   .   .   All is low,
> And false, and hollow—clay from first to last,
> The prince's urn no less than potter's vessel.
> .   .   .   So, we are slaves,
> The greatest as the meanest—nothing rests
> Upon our will, the will itself no less
> Depends upon a straw than on a storm;
> And when we think we lead, we are most led,
> And still towards death. . . .

This speech of the Doge's bears eloquent witness to the creative possibilities of skepticism, to the boundary skepticism shares with commitment when it is fully cognizant of itself. To define metaphysical study as "magic which recoils upon The adept who pursues it" befits a skeptic, but here does not denote one. Apparent skepticism in the Doge, instead of cutting him off from resolution and faith, makes a cause and support for a positive statement of values. The Doge Foscari is at once the stoic and the priest of the State.

The Two Foscari, in itself, countervails not only the extravagance of the heroic works but also the peculiarly defeated, even defeatist attitude of the mature satires. These also contain their own corrective. The opening stanzas of *The Vision of Judgment* graphically set up a framework of opposition to "great" men with the picture of "divine disgust" at "so many conquerors," and "at the crowning carnage, Waterloo." This opposition turns into revulsion with the picture of the devil "surfeited with the infernal revel" that "almost quenched his innate thirst of evil" (v-vi).

But it is left for *Don Juan*, in the cantos devoted to the Siege of Ismail, to make Byron's most complete and most profound statement of counter-heroic principles, specifically deflating the hero of mere power, specifically celebrating the life of courage and virtue. The very stanza that introduces the Siege warns us of the futility of the quest for what is "transcendent":

> O Love! O Glory! what are ye who fly
> Around us ever, rarely to alight?
> There's not a meteor in the polar sky
> Of such transcendent or more fleeting flight.
> Chill, and chained to cold earth, we lift on high
> Our eyes in search of either lovely light;
> A thousand and a thousand colours they
> Assume, then leave us on our freezing way.

Transcendent love having been dealt with, albeit some-what leniently, in the Juan-Julia and the Juan-Haidee episodes, the poem goes on to dissect the shining tumor of glory.[9] It does so, strikingly enough, with the same techniques that are associated with Byron's merry iconoclasm. Mordant rhymes and anticlimactic couplets do their work on Suwarrow and what he stands for, on War and what it entails. Byron performs at the top of his form manipulating Russian names, those in need of "pro-nunciation." The double meaning of names must be borne in mind here; Byron is talking about what one is called, and also about Chaucer's "pris," or how one is thought of as a reflection of one's mode of behavior and being. This ambiguity substantially enriches the entire stanza of names which he records,

> if but to increase
> Our euphony: there was Strongenoff and Strokonoff,
> Meknop, Serge Lwow, Arséniew of modern Greece,
> And Tschitsshakoff, and Roguenoff, and Chokenoff,
> And others of twelve consonants apiece;
> And more might be found out, if I could poke enough
> Into gazettes; but Fame (capricious strumpet),
> It seems, has got an ear as well as Trumpet.
>   (VII.xv)

The ironic idea of increasing euphony with the jaw-breaking roll call involves social and moral standards, and not just auditory ones. In Byron's unholy litany

---

[9] The separation is, of course, exaggerated in its strictness. Byron will go on, in the episode in the Russian Court, to show love and war as alternate manifestations of one personality, as conditions radiating from a single complex core. Ridenour aptly reminds us that in *Don Juan* "Love itself is seen as inextricably involved in violence" (*Style*, p. 71).

cacophony becomes one with evil; he must be renouncing, not just referring to "the common neoclassic notion that even the commonest and most vulgar utensils took on nobility in Greek" (Ridenour, *Style*, p. 135). Most of the "names" include and take the color of repugnant things: Tschitsshakoff, Roguenoff, and Chokenoff conveniently occur together. Whatever shred of the ordinary dignity of names may adhere to the likes of Strokonoff and Chokenoff gets blown away by the rhyme with the colloquially reductive "poke enough." On the other hand, whatever sympathy might go out to Fame for being moved to throw down her identifying trumpet—presumably she feels aesthetic distaste, but we also feel moral revulsion—is forestalled by the telling rhyme with "strumpet." Byron continually occupied himself with the labyrinthine implications of words and names. But here their volatility does not lead him to throw up his hands in helplessness, but is controlled to excoriate deserving victims.[10]

Rather than formal style, it is focus that changes in the War cantos. The change reflects a shift away from skep-

[10] The penetration and complexity of his response to "names" is commendable on philosophical as well as satirical grounds. Byron avoids the sad parochialism of disdaining a person because his name is unfamiliar or foreign. Such parochialism mars Boileau's "Fourth Epistle," with its merely aesthetic shuddering at "noms durs et barbares":

> Et qui peut, sans frémir, aborder Woërden?
> Quel vers ne tomberait au seul nom de Heusden?
> Quelle Muse, à rimer en tous lieux disposée
> Oserait approcher des bords de Zuiderzee?
> Comment, en vers heureux, assiéger Doësbourg,
> Zutphen, Wageninghen, Harderwic, Knotzembourg?

The retort of Prior in his "Epistle to Boileau" is richly deserved:

> Her warriors Anna sends from Tweed and Thames,
> That France may fall by more harmonious names.

tical, retracted satire to a more active, counter-heroic
satire, a shift which, incidentally, indicates the versatility of the seemingly mannered Byronic style. The result
is especially noteworthy in that these cantos show Byron
not only exposing human vice, but also honoring human
virtue.

The satire generally concerns itself with war, the
breeding ground of the "hero." The latter, the focal figure, is brought before us in three stages, with diminish-
ing distance and increasing intimacy. Within each stage,
too, a progression can be discerned, as Byron raises a
variety of points of view, each apparently independent,
each successive one however adjusting the one before
it with a definite downward impulse. To show this progression it will be necessary to give quotations at some
length. The hero is seen first in the abstract:

> . . . In approaching, were at length descried
> In this plain pair, Suwarrow and his guide.
>
> .   .   .   .   .
> . . . Great joy unto the camp!
> To Russian, Tartar, English, French, Cossacque,
> O'er whom Suwarrow shone like a gas lamp,
> Presaging a most luminous attack;
> Or like a wisp along the marsh so damp,
> Which leads beholders on a boggy walk,
> He flitted to and fro a dancing light,
> Which all who saw it followed, wrong or right.
>
> .   .   .   .   .
> 'T is thus the spirit of a single mind
> Makes that of multitudes take one direction,
> As roll the waters to the breathing wind,
> Or roams the herd beneath the bull's protection;

Or as a little dog will lead the blind,
Or a bell-wether form the flocks connection
By tinkling sounds, when they go forth to victual:
Such is the sway of your great men o'er little.

Here Suwarrow is a symbol, *the* leader, *felt* as leader. Twice his role would seem to merit the approbation of such as Carlyle, but in each case there is a violent readjustment of opinion: the apparently favorable image of the gas lamp yields to the cynical one of the will-o'-the-wisp; the appealing images of the wind gives place to ludicrous ones, the bull, the little seeing-eye dog, the bell-wether bent on eating. Byron is doing justice to the operation of heroic greatness, and violence to the principle of it.

Again, Suwarrow is brought before us in person, the hero in action:

Suwarrow chiefly was on the alert,
Surveying, drilling, ordering, jesting, pondering;
For the man was, we safely may assert,
A thing to wonder at beyond most wondering;
Hero, buffoon, half-demon and half-dirt,
Praying, instructing, desolating, plundering—
Now Mars, now Momus—and when bent to storm
A fortress, Harlequin in uniform.

The catalogue of Suwarrow's activities, "surveying" and so on, seems quite ordinary at first. But "jesting," which might bespeak adaptability and poise and a catholic mode of leadership (another Henry V, say), will take on derogatory value when he is called a buffoon. The whole catalogue, of course, is meant to be deceptive in its ordinariness, for paradox surrounds Suwarrow. He is man, and thing; wonderful, or perhaps rather egregious;

acceptable in praying and instructing, repellent in desolating and plundering. There is no mistaking what elements in this description should be seen as evidence of character, what as a matter of chance. Suwarrow, who lives as a hero, *is* a buffoon, with nothing of the angel, though something of the demon, about him, informing not his clay but his "dirt." His buffoon quality is reiterated and multiplied, as he becomes one with Momus[11] and Harlequin.

Such aspersions of the hero are given a certain corroboration when we see Suwarrow in a third, dramatic context, in the eyes of alien persons with alien susceptibilities. The "two Turkish ladies," who have befriended Juan and Johnson and who come with them into Suwarrow's camp, show us the hero in himself. Inevitably they see only the paltry man within the artificial—for them nonexistent—hero's cloak. Their reaction on finding that their lives are at his mercy is an object lesson in the adventitious nature of the hero state. For they, who are so skeptical of the seeing-eye dog of the giaours, see implicit Power in their own "imperial peacock." By a brilliant stroke on Byron's part, their incredulity and chagrin deflate both Suwarrow and their own exalted Sultan.

> . . . These two poor girls, with swimming eyes,
> Looked on as if in doubt if they could trust
> Their own protectors; nor was their surprise
> Less than their grief (and truly not less just)
> To see an old man, rather wild than wise
> In aspect, plainly clad, besmeared with dust,
> Stripped to his waistcoat, and that not too clean,
> More feared than all the Sultans ever seen.

[11] Here signifying not the spirit of mockery and blame, but susceptibility to that spirit.

For everything seemed resting on his nod,
As they could read in all eyes. Now to them,
Who were accustomed, as a sort of god,
To see the Sultan, rich in many a gem,
Like an imperial peacock stalk abroad
(That royal bird, whose tail's a diadem,)
With all the pomp of Power, it was a doubt
How Power could condescend to do without.

The translation of the Sultan into the ambience of a peacock, that emblem of vanity, and the equation of a diadem, that emblem of power, with the tail of the bird make for a deft and unmerciful devaluation. The military, and moral, distinction between Christian and pagan completely vanishes: the Sultan is as bad as Suwarrow. Byron, in sum, is assailing the concept of the hero, no matter where it holds sway. He is not performing a political hatchet-job. Suwarrow is not for him a personal aversion like Southey. Rather he makes a representative object of attack, the paramount figure in a dishonorable system that fosters "what story / Sometimes calls 'Murder,' and at others 'Glory.'"

Byron applies images of illusion and evanescence to the hero no less than to the glory he enjoys. The hero leads as a will-o'-the-wisp; glory is a meteor of "transcendent and fleeting flight," and shows in "fading twilight huses—so beautiful, so fleeting" (vii.lxxxii). In telling contrast, Byron stresses the perennial and universal quality of "the totality / Of deeds to human happiness most dear" (vii.lxxxiii), and of "honest fame" (viii.iii). The following stanzas typify this contrast and bring out, with unprecedented forthrightness, the radical defectiveness of the philosophy that enshrines the concept of heroism and glory:

History can only take things in the gross;
But could we take them in detail, perchance
In balancing the profit and the loss,
War's merit it by no means might enhance,
To waste so much gold for a little dross,
As hath been done, mere conquest to advance.
The drying up a single tear has more
Of honest fame, than shedding seas of gore.

And why?—because it brings self-approbation;
Whereas the other, after all its glare,
Shouts, bridges, arches, pensions from a nation,
Which (it may be) has not much left to spare,
A higher title, or a loftier station,
Though they may make Corruption gape or stare,
Yet, in the end, except in Freedom's battles,
Are nothing but a child of Murder's rattles.

Glory becomes equivalent to wantonness and murder.
It means perverted values—dross before gold—and
therefore the reduction of national strength as the moral
metaphor turns literal reality, with the nation put to it
to pay pensions. Corruption takes to it, but sanity (and
satire) will see that it stands opposed to generosity and
compassion and the spirit of freedom. After this one
truly is seized by the quietly mordant irony of the stanza
that begins, "Yet I love Glory. . . ."

Appreciation of Byron's twofold purpose, to depose
and also to propose models for conduct, contributes
substantially to a grasp of the Tartar Khan episode in the
Siege of Ismail (viii.civ.cxix). This episode provides a
multi-faceted dramatization of the philosophic principles
at work in the war cantos. The opposition between

"mere conquest" and a struggle for "Freedom" is fully etched here. In addition, the opposition that is possible between two outstanding actions, between true and vicious prowess, emerges to completement the contrast already seen of action, "shedding seas of gore," and compassion, "drying up a single tear." But more than mere opposition, the Tartar Khan episode brings about a confrontation of virtuous and corrupt heroism, with inspiring and poignant results. The latter finds itself unexpectedly "touched with a desire to shield and save," finds itself, to use Milton's phrase, "stupidly good." For a time it is not only physically thwarted but spiritually moved and chastened by the true heroism, whose beauty and superiority it, albeit purblindly, recognizes.

Byron's handling of the episode is sure and subtle. The fierce martial resolution of the "brave Tartar Khan" is tempered, for us, by his profound paternal love, and still enhanced as, unbroken, he beholds each of his five "brave sons" go down. The admiration his Christian enemies feel for him is qualified by their exasperation with him for retarding their conquest.

"To *take* him was the point.—" But he would *not* be *taken*, and replied

> To all the propositions of surrender
> By mowing Christians down on every side
> As obstinate as Swedish Charles at Bender.
> His five brave boys no less the foe defied;
> Whereon the Russian pathos grew less tender
> As being a virtue, like terrestrial patience,
> Apt to wear out on trifling provocations.
> .   .   .   .
> . . . All around were grown exceeding wroth
> At such a pertinacious infidel,

And poured upon him and his sons like rain,
Which they resisted like a sandy plain
That drinks and still is dry.
>   At last they perished. . . .

They perish one by one, and the Tartar Khan is soon alone. His death, I think, brings out the spiritual essence of strength and suffering, the superiority to accidents of number and position that Byron cryptically conveys in the death of the Gladiator in *Childe Harold* IV. There is something terrible about that death, in its pure will and courage, its seizure of silent anguish. Something even more terrible emerges from the fact that his slayers, though still "willing to concede / Quarter," and though "melted for a moment" at the end, presumably leap over his corpse to pursue their bloodthirsty business.[12] Their lust for glory ultimately inures them against what Byron meetly calls his "heroism," or, as in "The Siege of Corinth," his "stern exaltedness," though he is careful to stress that he is not "Describing Priam's, Peleus', or Jove's son," but "a good, plain, old, temperate man." Notwithstanding his prowess, the Tartar Khan is a hero of spirit, not of arms.

The soldiers who honor "his determined scorn of [merely material] life" do so with the volatile instinct of the soldier, without the comprehension that might lead to emulation. Juan, of course, in rescuing the "Moslem orphan" Leila, has already shown the capacity to put principles before the hot intoxication of mayhem and plunder. But Juan is no systematic hero, and cannot be

---

[12] Compare Byron's description of Bligh threatened by "the levelled muskets" of the mutineers: "Thou dar'st them to their worst, exclaiming 'Fire'! / But they who pitied not could yet admire."

such, in a world without precise, comprehensive principles. Some instinct, perhaps, makes him know how to die well, but not how to live well, makes him do well where artificial rules and forms break down (the shipwreck, the siege, the holdup on Shooter's Hill), but behave poorly, conventionally where they hold firm. His greatest removal from the tradition of the hero appears in his failure to grow into a substantial and stable consciousness of himself and his world. Byron does not make *him* see the kinship between cherishing Leila in her defenselessness and cherishing the Tartar Khan for defending his family and country. The impulses of war, Byron seems to say, are restrained only so well, and only so long. The saving of Leila is not an example but an anomaly, and, as Byron cries: "What's this in one annihilated city?" (viii.cxxiv). Though he usually appears quite noncommittal about Juan's character, he turns on him now and lances him with irony for his overall part in the battle (xxiv-xxv).[13]

It is repeatedly made clear throughout the cantos on the Siege of Ismail that Byron inveighs against war as the epitome of man-made ills. War represents (the anaphora is Hamletic in its dinning at evil):

[13] Alvin B. Kernan argues that there are "heavy and frequent attacks" on Juan throughout the poem (*The Plot of Satire*, pp. 201-202); likewise George M. Ridenour sees Juan being freely criticized, but only in the section on the Siege of Ismail. Such criticisms would raise less difficulty if, for example, Byron played up Juan's role as an interloping suitor during the Haidee episode, or as a hard assailant of the Tartar Khan during the Siege. But he does nothing of the kind; he distracts us from these possibilities by the way he speaks, or fails to speak, of Juan (see, by way of illustration, viii.lii, liv-lv, cviii-cix, cxl).

All that the mind would shrink from of excesses—
All that the body perpetrates of bad;
All that we read—hear—dream, of man's distresses—
All that the devil would do if run stark mad;
All that defies the worst which pen expresses,—
All by which Hell is peopled, or as sad
As Hell. . . .
           (VIII.cxxiii)

These cantos deal with a world differing in salient ways from that of the rest of *Don Juan*; the cardinal difference is to be found in the concentration on group or mob activity, and in the depiction of man as he is governed by an unexamined membership in a group. The presence of Leila, and of the Tartar Khan qualify this emphasis somewhat, but also point it up by contrast. The temper of the cantos is sharply altered, being freer and more forthright in dispraise and indignation. They could appear to enjoy a certain independence or even insularity in the complex structure of the poem, with a status that is conceivably one of obscure paradox, perhaps of inert contrast.

The opening stanzas of Canto IX, next after the Siege of Ismail, bring us squarely up against this difficulty. The berating of Wellington—"Villainton"—offers itself as a continuation, with a specifically English bearing, of the assault on Glory. But Byron abruptly turns, from such a strong statement of values and principles, back to a supine skepticism (xvi-xviii). After this shift, this relapse, he goes on to make his most sweeping avowal of his "plain, sworn, downright detestation / Of every despotism in every nation" (xxiv). Byron, I think, only seems to be weltering. He is moving quite surely and plausibly between the poles of idealistic indignation and practical resignation. His detestation of despotism breaks out of control, or into the open, only with respect to the ultimate despotism, war of conquest. His skeptical reluctance to hold up standards has its limits here. He ceases, here, to have the control, or callousness, to say merely that "such things are."

Byron gives warning of this alteration of manner at the very threshold of the War Cantos, where he springs on the reader with sudden and unparalleled bluntness and animosity:

> In this scene of all confess'd inanity,
> By Saint, by Sage, by Preacher, and by Poet
> Must I restrain me, through the fear of strife,
> From holding up the nothingness of Life?
>
> Dogs, or men!—for I flatter you in saying
> That ye are dogs—your betters far—ye may
> Read, or read not, what I am now essaying
> To show you what ye are in every way.
> As little as the moon stops for the baying
> Of wolves, will the bright Muse withdraw one ray
> From out her skies—then howl your idle wrath!
> While she still silvers o'er your gloomy path.
>   (vii.vi, 5-vii)

And yet, after clearly planning the sort of selfless, unbuttoned attack on monstrous humanity which has just been described, after recognizing that it was "necessary, in the present clash of philosophy and tyranny, to throw away the scabbard" (LJ, vi, 101), he might seem to have forgotten his aim far enough to give way to gratuitous scurrility, in the matter of the Moorish women who lament their not being taken as the first perquisites of the Russian victory. This would be a rather surprising departure from the prevailing spirit of the War Cantos, and it seems likely that the passage has been misjudged, even by Byron's most sympathetic critics.[14] Both the context in which he brings up the frustrated females and an analogous passage from Dryden's *The Spanish Friar* support the view that Byron is not indulging a lubricous taste, but an indignant distaste for certain anomalies in human conduct.

The relevant passage from *The Spanish Friar* occurs at the end of a battle between Christians and Moors— also the combatants in *Don Juan*—but the besiegers, the Moors, have been repulsed. Lorenzo, a stalwart in the defense of the city, is surprised to find himself anything but a hero in the eyes of his countrywomen:

> I have been ranging over half the town; but have
> sprung no game. Our women are worse infidels
> than the Moors; I told them I was one of the
> knight-errants, that delivered them from ravish-
> ment; and I think in my conscience, that is their
> quarrel to me.
> (I.ii)[15]

No specific person is involved in *Don Juan* (VIII.cxxviii); but there is a similar urgent sense of ugly aberration in the women. Byron is asking us to shudder, not snigger.

---

[14] Rutherford, for example, deems it "cynically flippant," a case of "frivolous bad taste," and again "an upsurge of rakish cynicism" (*Byron: A Critical Study*, pp. 178-179); Joseph sees it as "perhaps the only lapse in human understanding in the whole poem" (*Byron the Poet*, p. 280); and Ridenour comes down on it as "rather tasteless humor" (*Style*, p. 71).

[15] *The Spanish Friar, or, The Double Discovery*, quoted from *The Works of John Dryden*, ed. Sir Walter Scott, rev. and corr. by George Saintsbury, vol. VI, Edinburgh, 1898.

Moreover, the women's petulant query, "Wherefore the ravishing did not begin!" (cxxxii), is subtly integrated into the main discussion of the Siege. Supposedly it goes to prove how "chaste" the Russian troops were in victory, and therefore how fit to be praised. But can any praise seem less than narrow and prurient if we weigh the enormity of massacre against continence that turns out to be accidental? What made the Russians "chaste" looks as transient as the effect of cold or hunger and fatigue (cxxviii). If their "chastity" has a more permanent source, it is in the predominance of bloodthirstiness or greed in their makeup: "while [their] thirst for gore and plunder raged, / There was small leisure for superfluous sin" (cxxxii). The announced theme of praise is subverted by its own evidence, and leads against its own interest to a reaction of amusement and then aversion. On this reading an almost Swiftian irony develops in the sex-oriented finale of the Siege, making it trenchant, not out of place, a further statement of "detestation," not a tasteless aside. It is a vital part of Byron's "sustained attempt at realism in all aspects of the story. Plot, incident, description, character-portrayal, and the poet's own attitude to his narration, were all to be governed by fidelity to truth—by his knowledge of things as they really are" (Rutherford, pp. 168-169).

The ultimate unsuitableness of a course that might have set better with a delicate and discreet audience stands out clearly when we consider John Hookham Frere's more "correct" version of the issue of a decisive battle, in *The Monks and the Giants*; it is one of the many material points of technique, tone, and conception where Byron strides independently away from this elementary "model" for his great comic verse. Frere's treatment of

THE LIMITS OF SKEPTICISM

the actual hostilities, let us recall, is deliberately shy. The battle as well as the participants in it are observed from a carefully chosen "station . . . that's picturesque and perfectly secure." The result is a comfortable fantasy, with a sprinkling of gory levity wholly detached from the implications of war as such. In sharp contrast the basic seriousness and reflective power of Byron's view of war bulk through the comic appearances of the con-frontation between Satan and Saint Michael in *The Vision of Judgment,* and take on an uncompromising fullness and clarity in the Siege of Ismail in *Don Juan.* Consistent with his peculiar approach, Frere after the giants' defeat has his victorious knights worrying over the possible fate of the ladies whom the giants had held captive. The narrator interposes with the assurance that

They were tolerably well,
At least as well as could have been expected;
Many details I must forbear to tell,
Their toilet had been very much neglected;
But by supreme good luck it so befell
That when the Castle's capture was effected,
When those vile cannibals were overpower'd,
Only two fat Duennas were devour'd.

This may represent the good-natured, polite version of the way sieges end, but it is not unexceptionable; in fact it entails a certain artistic dishonesty and unctuousness. One discerns the cute leer of pious reassurance as the un-mistakable suggestion of sex is turned off into something more innocuous, dress, or more improbable and taste-less, cannibalism. Indeed, the latter idea is gratuitously slipped into the poem, and amounts to a deplorable aspersion of the lusty giants who had earlier abducted the ladies like so many Sabines. Frere doubtless meant to eschew the indecency for which he was to think *Don Juan* deserved to be suppressed. Yet he becomes guilty of another indecency, and he foregoes the substance contained in Byron's canvassing of such questions as the nature of war, of women, of adventitious chastity, of reputation and praise. He suppresses moral concern in favor of a moralistic delicacy, and opens himself to the charge of being insensitively bland and playful about that area of human experience which moves the supposedly unprincipled Byron to such keen indignation.

This moral feeling of detestation is not otherwise nullified. On the contrary, it must be no more than dissimulated by the urbane, sardonic, amoral air of *Beppo* and the greater part of *Don Juan*. And that air must be subtly modified in the directions of a greater strictness by Byron's "sworn, downright detestation of *every* despotism in *every* nation." In personal relationships the despotism of Donna Inez, who, not content with such unfeeling advantage of Juan and Julia, goes complacently sailing from generation to generation with her pedagogy, trailing ruin in her wake; the more patent despotism of Lambro (surely some criticism is reflected on Lambro in the "long low island song / Of ancient days, ere tyranny grew strong," iv.lxv); that of Gulbeyaz and of the Empress Catherine, in the twilight zone of love and politics; of Wellington and Castlereagh in the political realm, as of Wordsworth, Coleridge, and Southey in the literary and intellectual realm; the despotism of good intentions in Lady Adeline, who seeks to manipulate the lives of Juan and Aurora; perhaps even the despotism of the unchaste Laura over the inarticulate Beppo: all would seem to come under his comprehensive anathema.

Instead of Byron's "rage" being "absorbed into and to some extent neutralized by the . . . comic perspective" (Bostetter, p. 282), the satire of *Don Juan*, Byronic satire may be at bottom something less than forebearing. Perhaps, indeed, in some of the last lines penned by him, Byron holds out a canny analysis of his temper:

> Just as I make my mind up every day,
> To be a '*Totus, teres*,' Stoic, Sage,
> The wind shifts and I fly into a rage.

Here is instinct surging free of resolution, subverting it, bringing to light the difficulties and dissimulations of its calm. And this self-conception is evinced as early as 1817, when Byron had written: "I am a quiet man, like Candide, though with somewhat of his fortune in being forced to forego my natural meekness now and then" (*LJ*, IV, 146).

Just as the counter-heroic elements in *Don Juan* virtually produce a chemical change in that poem, the counter-heroic drama, *The Two Foscari*, reflects a new light on the sense of values that passes current in the regular plays. A latent criticism of the self-centered attitude of the protagonist—be his position private or political—is perceptible even within the "heroic" works, especially *Sardanapalus* and *Manfred* and *Cain*. In principle, that criticism is given full utterance in *The Two Foscari*, inasmuch as this play generates a spirit of austere, self-sacrificing humanism and patriotism, though it preserves "classical" form and quasi-heroic features. One wonders if this relation may not, beyond simply reflecting on the indulgence of self-will in Byron's heroic works, also serve to refocus it. Certainly, the stern counter-heroic was the only possible, and the only appropriate, position to affirm against the negative *Weltansicht* that is implicit in the heroic and the idio-satirical works.

Conceivably it comes as a necessary development therefrom. It is arresting to see Byron turning all but the very words of pessimism into the language of acceptance and endurance. "Stanzas for Music (They say that Hope is happiness)" ends with the gripping lines:

> Alas! it is delusion all;
> The future cheats us from afar,
> Nor can we be what we recall,
> Nor dare we think on what we are.

But in *Childe Harold* (iii.cxi), less than two years later, Byron sees more in the same future, and present, and past, and so sees otherwise:

> To feel
> We are not what we have been, and to deem
> We are not what we should be, and to steel
> The heart against itself; and to conceal
> With a proud caution, love, or hate, or aught,—
> Passion or feeling, purpose, grief, or zeal,—
> Which is the tyrant spirit of our thought,
> Is a stern task of soul;—no matter—it is taught.

It may be too much to aver that Byron wholly repudiated the view: "it is delusion all." Rather I think he contended with its crippling implications and learned, or was taught, in his own richly oxymoronic phrase, "a proud caution." Skeptic and zealot, he recognizes, if he does not faithfully devote himself to, the "stern task of soul."

It can be readily observed that Byron does not develop the principle of stoicism, as in the birthday lyric for his thirty-sixth year, without also giving his countenance to what may be the blind side of stoicism, namely sentimentality, or a partial faith in the availability of the heart's desire. Doubtless his was not St. Anselm's faith—*fides quaerens intelligentiam.* But the problem of possible faith continually and embarrassingly going aground on the shoals of intelligence—the pattern incarnate in the Byronic ottava rima stanza—perceptibly lessened in severity for him. If a pressure toward comprehension becomes paramount in *Childe Harold* IV and the greater part of *Don Juan*, and a pressure toward order in *The Two Foscari* and the key Tartar Khan episode in *Don Juan*, a relaxation or resolution of pressure also becomes apparent in an assortment of later works. Not that we should look for a resolution in the formal terms of a philosophical position; the change operates in the spirit of an existential choice. Thus, perhaps, Matthew Arnold might contend that Byron's "intellectual deliverance" is not perfect, that he falls short of "that harmonious acquiescence of mind which we feel in contemplating a grand spectacle that is intelligible to us."[16] But the reasons for such a failing lie in contradictory directions: Byron does not find or render the grand spectacle quite intelligible, and, on the other hand, he does not subside into the quietist passivity of acquiescence. What we see in him amounts to a combination of intellectual candor and active personal commitment.

The appearance of this combination is not sudden; it has been earlier intimated in *Childe Harold* IV, in the

---

[16] "On the Classical Tradition," in *The Complete Prose of Matthew Arnold*, 4 vols., ed. R. H. Super, Ann Arbor, Michigan, 1960, I, 20.

decision to "ponder boldly" (st. cxxvii). With the qualifying word, boldly, a mood of courage and implicit hope
arises to color the impersonal and impassive act of pondering. The power of the individual mind gets its temper
from the power of the individual spirit, because the qual-
ifier truly works to determine the quality of the thing it
is associated with. In other words Byron manages to fuse
the two responses necessary "in presence of an immense,
moving, confused spectacle which, while it perpetually
excites our curiosity, perpetually baffles our comprehension."[17] He considers its nature (ponder), and he affirms
his stance in relation to it (boldly).

The active mental and moral state telescoped into the
phrase "ponder boldly" is nowhere more substantially
displayed than in Byron's last major work, *The Island*,
as he candidly sets forth irreconcilable claims of order
and impulse and, abandoning any pretense at a unifying
philosophy, creates in Torquil a naïve beneficiary of the
conflict, to whom is made an award of happiness. With
happiness rather than order or understanding as the
touchstone of choice, feeling and personality gain a distinct ascendancy over discursive and deliberate judgment in the scheme of things, and it is remarkable that
the emphasis on happiness reiterates that of the early
romantic lyrics; Byron as it were purposefully espouses
what had spontaneously drawn him before. Though no
sensible argument offers itself to uphold the possibility that this is Byron's last (and not just latest) orientation, much may be made of it in the overall complex of
his poetry.

That poetry has as its inclusive issue, against which
any other is likely to be originally or ultimately studied,

[17] *Ibid.*

the issue of time. Clearly the problems of the experience of time pervade the romantic period, and practically furnish one of its defining terms;[18] for romantic poetry the history of radical losses in the life of the spirit, losses in and really also to time, stands without need of documentary props, as do the proofs of "abundant recompense" and cardinal hopes of "something evermore about to be." But Byron remains noteworthy as the most persistent, the most analytical, and the most philosophically intricate of the romantics in attacking time's long design. The quality and the terms of his attack have partially emerged in the process of considering his romantic lyrics as well as the workings of structure, imagery, and allusion in his poetry. Here, beyond recalling what has been brought out, we may usefully confront a further passage, the opening stanzas of *Don Juan* x, with time as the primary focus; the explicit authorial statement, half-comic in its scheme of redemption and half-ironic in its self-assertion, constitutes a significant forecast, in orbit around the central theme of time, of the combined candor (confessed limitation) and commitment (professed choice) in *The Island*.

The stanzas in question (x.i-iv) set up a triangular relationship among science or scientific discovery, poetry, and the stars—the apex of the triangle; one finds also a subordinate link between attaining the stars, an upward act, and sailing against the wind, an outward act, as examples of going counter to the given, and, by transcending normal limitations, redefining and redeeming

[18] As Frederick Garber observes in his article, "Wordsworth and the Romantic Synecdoche," "consciousness of movement, of the effects of time and flux, was at least as pervasive and agonizing as the similar pattern in Renaissance poetry" (*Bucknell Review*, xiv [1966], 36).

the possibilities of human nature and experience. Critical episodes in the history of man and the universe make up the subject of the lines: the Fall, and, implicitly after a sad interval of privation, a new discovery or recovery in the form of Newtonian physics. The statement of the lines seems to be that poetry can and should in its sphere do the equivalent of what physics has done (in particular Byron's poetry is tackling this task, and defiantly is said to be equal to it). The lines need to be read straightforwardly; this has been done by critics as alert as Ridenour and Joseph. But it is necessary also to acknowledge in them an undertone of irony and not unfriendly amusement. The passage overall seems less optimistic or celebrative than lucidly and gracefully determined.

Certain indices of levity or of tentativeness seem salient enough: the deflating idea of the spirit's "cutting a caper," or of the "turnpike road" of the stars, or of reputedly immortal man glowing "with all kinds of mechanics"; and concessive verbs like "must deem," "would skim," "may float," to say nothing of the forthright refusal to "answer . . . for any sage's creed or calculation." Beyond the refusal to trust either faith or arithmetic, one observes that the chiasmus fell-apple-apple-rose fails to distinguish between mechanics and morality, or the literal and figurative senses of the word 'fall.' The rhetorical balance only formally betrays the conceptual disparity. Correspondingly the logical counters in the second stanza (if, for, must) help to reveal illogical assumptions and deductions, not the least of which would be the equation of redemption with a trip to the moon. As Horace might have said: *coelum non animum mutant qui in lunam currunt.* Throughout the passage

there is a disjunction between objective and means, desire and capability, and Byron insists on the disjunction
even while sympathizing with the objective.

His attitude toward himself carries to its culmination
the mixture of energetic hope and unquestioned limitation: "though so much inferior, as I know, . . . I wish to
do as much by poesy." The fourth and final stanza of
this brief sally into historical and biographical philosophy has as its characteristic movement a swinging between assertion ("in the wind's eye I have sail'd, and
sail") and disclaimer ("but for / The stars, I own my
telescope is dim"), between active desire and light,
strong movement ("would skim") and heavy, passive motion ("may float"). Byron appears as more dreamer than
hero, even if his dreams have a heroic tinge.

As regards both the method and the content of *Don
Juan* he may of course claim to be sailing in the wind's
eye. But a more glamorous or cosmic reading of the passage scarcely seems justified. It is of moment that Byron
at first equates discovering stars and sailing in the
wind's eye, then disunites the two in his own case and
rules out the vertical or star-seeking action, though it
would seem the likelier one to have kept in view of his
reference to Newton and the Fall. It is evident, though,
that he means to emphasize general exploration over specific aspiration. The end of the ninth canto has clearly
confessed that Byron has no head for heights, if also no
taste for being stationed and earthbound. Chiming with
this view, in the tenth canto Byron does more searching
than soaring. To be sure, exploration has definite value,
as a negation of smugness and inertia, but without pre-
suming any final goal or final success. Nor does the nature of his act require exaggeration to merit admiration.

For Byron is making a deliberate choice of exploration, an act of spirit as much as of intellect, and thus ethically free despite its practical uncertainties.

The system of exploration does not appear so absolute as to reject a graft of acceptance and resolution; in fact it promotes it, and we have seen it dramatized in *The Two Foscari* and the Siege of Ismail in *Don Juan*. "On This Day I Complete My Thirty-Sixth Year" makes a formal principle of resolution and acceptance, recanting a memorable profession of hedonism in Byron's past:

> I once thought myself a philosopher, and talked nonsense [resolution and acceptance?] with great decorum: I defied pain, and preached up equanimity. For some time this did very well, for no one was in *pain* for me but my friends, and none lost their patience but my hearers. At last, a fall from my horse convinced me bodily suffering was an evil; and the worst of an argument overset my maxims and my temper at the same moment; so I quitted Zeno for Aristippus, and conceive that pleasure constitutes the *TO KALON*.

Perhaps Byron's full position—his ideal and his relation to it—has its summary in his remark to Thomas Moore: "I have been all my life trying to harden my heart,[19] and have not yet quite succeeded" (*LJ*, III, 92). This is the implied attitude of "Stanzas to the Po," which though it seems to foster tumult, or to despair of peace, actually insists on the unmoved, stoical state insofar as it fancies even death ("let me perish young") as a way out of helpless agitation ("live as I lived, and love as I loved").

---

[19] In the direction of stoicism, and without intimations of cruelty.

Some sort of rebellious treatment of facts, exemplified in a poem like "Aristomenes" with its Keatsian nostalgia for an indubitably dead divinity, persists to the last in Byron's writing; and some sort of instability and incontinence appears, as in the more than avuncular affection of the piece commonly entitled "Love and Death." But these are tangents to the prevailing curve of his final work. Indeed "Aristomenes" is modulated subtly enough to reveal, along with a resistance to historical fact, a submission to emotional reality—the basic need of a divine mythos is confessed, even as it is agreed that one finds no cultural basis for fulfilling that need. Because it is lucidly, even humbly chosen, the surrender of the emotions to the myth of the gods takes on its own philosophical validity.

The presence of a choice made in this lucid, humble spirit appears as a paramount development in Byron's final work. By it idealism is rendered somehow practical and enabled to foil the thrusts of analytical aspirituality. Accordingly special attention is due *The Island*, with its serene passage between the threatening rock of social order and the treacherous pool of individual preference. As already remarked, no attempt is made at a reconciliation. The facts stand: mutiny is abhorrent; so is its punishment. The salient feature of the "paradox Paradise of Toobonai," as Blackstone aptly describes it (*Lost Travellers*, p. 219), is that Byron sees it as such, and rather than not have it boldly chooses to have it so. Only on the surface does this betray an "urge to regress to an infantile state of irresponsibility" (Blackstone, p. 212). For their responsibility, or rather the (perilous) absolution from responsibility gained by Torquil and Neuha in their natural "sanctuary" is not shared by Byron, though it is favored by him as something one can save from a wideflung establishment of order and retribution; the collapse of order, instead of meaning total chaos, may yield or lead to an island of happiness. Moreover, this absolution from responsibility is not available to Christian, or to anyone less remote from the guilty mutiny than Torquil. (In the same vein evasion of responsibility breeds monsters in *Werner*, which is ominously subtitled "The Inheritance," and a self-seeking pursuit of happiness in *The Deformed Transformed* proves no less grotesque in its consequences.) Byron's sentimentality does not benefit the criminal or, more important, himself. Happiness for Torquil and Neuha in *The Island* coexists with self-denial and stoicism for himself, as in "On This Day I Complete My Thirty-Sixth Year."

Psychologically and morally this resembles the time-honored position of charitable asceticism. One wonders whether Byron would have further consolidated and articulated this position; certainly its possibilities for poetry could have been more substantially and grippingly given than in *The Island*. But even there catholicity of attention lessens the partiality of the conclusion, which in justice needs to be appreciated as a matter of character and choice, and not logic. More than "an extraordinary personal confession" or "the poet's last desperate articulation of hope for man,"[20] it achieves and professes a certain psychic health. In the simplicity of Byron's affection for the "happy days" of Torquil and Neuha, his acknowledgment of Bligh's integrity as a champion of dutiful ways, and his growing acceptance of an ennobling severity in his treatment of himself, one

[20] Robert F. Gleckner, *Byron and the Ruins of Paradise*, p. 350.

recognizes a fertile combination whose fruit was denied by the prophylaxis of death. Byron, we know, died at thirty-six. And it remains beguilingly poignant to reflect that he had once, not altogether playfully perhaps, imagined thirty-six as the age at which he would have embarked on the life of perfection.

BIBLIOGRAPHY

Abrams, M. H. "Structure and Style in the Greater Romantic Lyric," in *From Sensibility to Romanticism*, ed. Frederick W. Hilles and Harold Bloom. New Haven, 1965.

Amarasingle, Upali. *Dryden and Pope in the Early Nineteenth Century: A Study of Changing Literary Taste*, 1800-1830. Cambridge, 1962.

Arnold, Matthew. "Byron," in *Essays in Criticism*, 2nd ser. London, 1888.

————. *The Complete Prose*. 4 vols., ed. R. H. Super. Ann Arbor, Michigan, 1960.

Bate, Walter Jackson. *John Keats*. Cambridge, Mass., 1963.

Baumer, Franklin L. *Religion and the Rise of Scepticism*. New York, 1960.

Beers, Henry A. *A History of English Romanticism in the Eighteenth Century*. New York, 1899.

Blackstone, Bernard. *The Lost Travellers; A Romantic Theme with Variations*. London, 1962.

Blake, William. *The Poetry and Prose*, ed. David V. Erdman with commentary by Harold Bloom. New York, 1965.

Blessington, Countess of. *Conversations of Lord Byron with the Countess of Blessington*, 2nd edn. London, 1850.

Bloom, Harold. "Keats and the Embarrassments of Poetic Tradition," in *From Sensibility to Romanticism*, ed. Frederick W. Hilles and Harold Bloom. New Haven, 1965.

————. *The Visionary Company*. New York, 1963.

Borst, William A. *Lord Byron's First Pilgrimage*. New Haven, 1948.

Bostetter, Edward Everett. *The Romantic Ventriloquists: Wordsworth, Coleridge, Keats, Shelley, Byron*. Seattle, Wash., 1963.

Boyd, Elizabeth French. *Byron's Don Juan: A Critical Study*. New Brunswick, New Jersey, 1945.

Brett-Smith, H.F.B., ed. *Peacock's Four Ages of Poetry, Shelley's Defence of Poetry, Browning's Essay on Shelley*. Oxford, 1921.

Bruffee, Kenneth A. "The Synthetic Hero and the Narrative Structure of *Childe Harold* III." *SEL*, VI (1966), 669-678.

Byron, George Gordon, Lord. *Byron's Don Juan: A Variorum Edition*, eds. Truman Guy Steffan and Willis W. Pratt. 4 vols. Austin, Texas, 1957.

————. *The Complete Poetical Works*. Cambridge edn., ed. Paul Elmer More. Boston, 1905.

————. *The Poetical Works. The Only Complete and Copyright Text in One Volume*, ed. with a Memoir by Ernest Hartley Coleridge. London, 1905.

————. *Selected Letters*, ed. with an intro. by Jacques Barzun. New York, 1953.

————. *The Selected Poetry*, ed. with an intro. by Leslie A. Marchand. New York, 1951.

————. *The Works. Letters and Journals*, ed. Rowland E. Prothero. 6 vols. London, 1898-1901.

————. *The Works. Poetry*, ed. Ernest Hartley Coleridge. 7 vols. London, 1898-1905.

Calvert, William J. *Byron: Romantic Paradox*. Chapel Hill, North Carolina, 1935.

Carlyle, Thomas. *On Heroes, Hero-Worship, and the Heroic in History*, ed. Archibald MacMechan. New York, 1901.

Chew, Samuel C. *The Dramas of Lord Byron*. Göttingen 1915.

————. "The Nineteenth Century and After," in *A Literary History of England*, ed. Albert C. Baugh. New York, 1948.

————. *The Relation of Lord Byron to the Drama of the Romantic Period*. Baltimore, Maryland, 1914.

Coleridge, Samuel Taylor. *Collected Letters*, ed. Earl Leslie Griggs. 4 vols. Oxford, 1956-59.

————. *Biographia Literaria*, ed. with his Aesthetical Essays by J. Shawcross. 2 vols. Oxford, 1907.

————. *The Complete Poetical Works, including Poems and Versions of Poems Now Published for the First Time*, ed. with textual and bibliographical notes by Ernest Hartley Coleridge. 2 vols. Oxford, 1957.

Colie, R. L. "The Rhetoric of Transcendence." *PQ*, XLIII (1964), 145-170.

Davie, Donald. *Purity of Diction in English Verse*. New York, 1953.

[D'Israeli, Isaac]. "Spence's *Anecdotes of Books and Men*." *Quarterly Review*, XXIII (1820), 400-434.

'Don John' or Don Juan Unmasked: being a key to the mystery attending that remarkable publication; with a descriptive review of the poem, and extracts. London, 1819.

Dryden, John. *The Works*. Illustrated with notes, historical, critical, and explanatory, and a life of the author, by Sir Walter Scott, bart. Rev. and corr. by George Saintsbury. Vol. VI. Edinburgh, 1893.

Du Bos, Charles. *Byron and the Need of Fatality*, trans. by Ethel C. Mayne. London, 1932.

Eckhardt, Eduard. "Lord Byrons komische Reime." *Englische Studien*, LXX (1936), 198-208.

Eliot, T. S. "Byron," in *From Anne To Victoria, Essays by Various Hands*, ed. Bonamy Dobrée. London, 1937.

Elliott, G. R. "Byron and the Comic Spirit." *PMLA*, XXXIX (1924), 897-909.

Elton, Oliver. *A Survey of English Literature: 1780-1830*. Vol. II. London, 1912.

Evans, B. Ifor. "Manfred's Remorse and Dramatic Tradition."
PMLA, LXII (1947), 752-773.
Fogle, Richard Harter. "A Note on Romantic Oppositions and Reconciliations," in *The Major English Romantic Poets: A Symposium in Reappraisal*, eds. Clarence D. Thorpe et al. Carbondale, Illinois, 1957.
Frye, Northrop. *Anatomy of Criticism: Four Essays*. Princeton, New Jersey, 1957.
————. *Fables of Identity: Studies in Poetic Mythology*. New York, 1963.
Garber, Frederick. "Wordsworth and the Romantic Synecdoche," *Bucknell Review*, XIV (1966), 33-43.
Gleckner, Robert F. *Byron and the Ruins of Paradise*. Baltimore, Maryland, 1967.
Goode, Clement Tyson. *Byron as Critic*. Weimar, 1923.
Gray, Thomas. *The Works . . . in Prose and Verse*, ed. Edmund Gosse. 4 vols. London, 1903.
Grierson, H.J.C. *The Background of English Literature and Other Collected Essays and Addresses*. London, 1925.
————. *Lyrical Poetry from Blake to Hardy*. London, 1928.
Harrison, John William. "The Imagery of Byron's Romantic Narratives and Dramas." Univ. of Colorado Ph.D. thesis, 1958; L.C. Card: Mic 59-829.
Hartman, Geoffrey H. "Wordsworth, Inscriptions, and Romantic Nature Poetry," in *From Sensibility to Romanticism*, eds. Frederick W. Hilles and Harold Bloom. New Haven, 1965.
Hassler, Donald M. "*Marino Faliero*, the Byronic Hero, and *Don Juan*." *K-SJ*, XIV (1965), 55-64.
Hazlitt, William. *The Spirit of the Age*. In *The Complete Works*, ed. P. P. Howe after the edition of A. R. Waller and Arnold Glover. Vol. XI. London, 1930.
————. *Literary and Political Criticism*. In *The Complete Works*, ed. P. P. Howe. . . . Vol. XIX. London, 1930.
————. *Lectures on the English Comic Writers*. London, 1819.
[Heber, R.] "Lord Byron's Dramas." *Quarterly Review*, XXVII (1822), 476-524.
Hirsch, E. D., Jr. "Byron and the Terrestrial Paradise," in *From Sensibility to Romanticism*, eds. Frederick W. Hilles and Harold Bloom. New Haven, 1965.
Hollander, John. *The Untuning of the Sky: Ideas of Music in English Poetry, 1500-1700*. Princeton, New Jersey, 1961.
Horn, András. *Byron's "Don Juan" and the Eighteenth-Century English Novel*. Bern, Switzerland, 1962.
Jack, Ian. *English Litrature 1815-1832. The Oxford History of English Literature*. Vol. X. Oxford, 1963.
[Jeffrey, Francis.] "Lord Byron's Poetry." *Edinburgh Review*, XXVII (1816), 277-310.

———. "Lord Byron's Tragedies." *Edinburgh Review,* xxxvi (1822), 413-452.
Johnson, Edward Dudley Hume. "Don Juan in England." *ELH,* xi (1944), 135-153.
Joseph, M. K. *Byron the Poet.* London, 1964.
Keats, John. *The Letters,* 1814-1821, ed. Hyder Edward Rollins. 2 vols. Cambridge, Mass., 1958.
———. *The Poetical Works,* ed. with an intro. and textual notes by H. Buxton Forman. Oxford, 1931.
Kernan, Alvin B. *The Plot of Satire.* New Haven, 1965.
Knight, G. Wilson. *The Burning Oracle: Studies in the Poetry of Action.* Oxford, 1939.
———. *Byron and Shakespeare.* New York, 1966.
———. *The Starlit Dome: Studies in the Poetry of Vision.* London, 1941.
Kroeber, Karl. *Romantic Narrative Art.* Madison, Wisconsin, 1960.
Le Bossu, René. *Treatise of the Epick Poem, Containing Many Curious Reflections Very Useful for the Right Understanding and Judging of the Excellencies of Homer and Virgil.* Trans. with a preface by W. J., 2nd edn. Vol. i. London, 1719.
Lindenberger, Herbert. *On Wordsworth's Prelude.* Princeton, New Jersey, 1963.
Lockhart, John Gibson. *John Bull's Letter to Lord Byron,* ed. Alan Lang Strout. Norman, Oklahoma, 1947.
"Lord Byron's *Hebrew Melodies.*" *Analectic Magazine,* vi (1815), 292-294.
———. *Christian Observer,* xiv (1815), 542-549.
Lovell Ernest J., Jr. *Byron: The Record of a Quest: Studies in a Poet's Concept and Treatment of Nature.* Austin, Texas, 1949.
———. ed. *His Very Self and Voice.* New York, 1954.
———. "Irony and Image in *Don Juan,*" in *English Romantic* New Jersey, 1966.
———. ed. *Medwin's Conversations of Lord Byron.* Princeton, *Poets: Modern Essays in Criticism,* ed. M. H. Abrams. Galaxy Book. New York, 1960.
Lyon, Judson S. "Romantic Psychology and the Inner Senses: Coleridge." *PMLA,* lxxxi (1966), 246-260.
Marchand, Leslie A. *Byron: A Biography.* 3 vols. New York, 1957.
———. "Byron and the Modern Spirit," in *The Major English Romantic Poets: A Symposium in Reappraisal,* eds. Clarence D. Thorpe et al. Carbondale, Illinois, 1957.
Marshall, William H. *The Structure of Byron's Major Poems.* Philadelphia, Pennsylvania, 1962.
Martin, L. C. *Byron's Lyrics.* Byron Foundation Lecture, 1948. Nottingham, n.d.
Mayo, Robert. "The Contemporaneity of the Lyrical Ballads." *PMLA,* lxix (1954), 486-522.

Medwin, Thomas. *Conversations of Lord Byron*. 2 vols. in one. London, 1832.

Millar, John. "On Wit and Humour." *Blackwood's Edinburgh Magazine*, VI (1820), 638-642.

Morley, John. "Byron." *Fortnightly Review*, VIII NS (1870), 650-673.

Moore, Thomas. *Letters and Journals of Lord Byron, with Notices of His Life*. 3rd edn. 3 vols. London, 1833.

Muir, Kenneth, ed. *Elizabethan Lyrics*. New York, 1953.

Murray, John, ed. *Lord Byron's Correspondence, chiefly with Lady Melbourne, Mr. Hobhouse, the Hon. Douglas Kinnaird, and P. B. Shelley*. 2 vols. London, 1922.

Nathan, Isaac. *Fugitive Pieces and Reminiscences of Lord Byron, containing an Entire New Edition of the Hebrew Melodies, with the Addition of Several Never before Published*. London, 1829.

Pafford, Ward. "Byron and the Mind of Man: *Childe Harold* III-IV and *Manfred*." *SiR*, I (Winter 1962), 105-128.

Peckham, Morse. *Beyond the Tragic Vision: The Quest for Identity in the Nineteenth Century*. New York, 1962.

————. "Toward a Theory of Romanticism: II Reconsiderations." *SiR*, I (Autumn 1961), 1-8.

Pönitz, Arthur. *Byron und die Bibel*. Leipzig, 1906.

Pratt, Willis W. "Byron and Some Current Patterns of Thought," in *The Major Romantic Poets: A Symposium in Reappraisal*, eds. Clarence D. Thorpe et al. Carbondale, Illinois, 1957.

Quennell, Peter, ed. *Byron: A Self-Portrait*. 2 vols. London, 1950.

————. *Byron in Italy*. New York, 1941.

————. *Byron: The Years of Fame*. New York, 1935.

Rebec, George. "Byron and Morals." *International Journal of Ethics*, XIV (1904), 39-54.

Ridenour, George. "Byron and the Romantic Pilgrimage: A Critical Examination of the Third and Fourth Cantos of *Childe Harold's Pilgrimage*." Unpublished dissertation (Yale, 1955).

————. "Byron in 1816: Four Poems from Diodati," in *From Sensibility to Romanticism*, eds. Frederick W. Hilles and Harold Bloom, New Haven, 1965.

————. *The Style of Don Juan*. New Haven, 1960.

Rougemont, Denis de. *Love in the Western World*, trans. by Montgomery Belgion, rev. and augmented edn. New York, 1956.

Ruskin, John. *Praeterita*. In *The Works of John Ruskin*, ed. E. T. Cook and Alexander Wedderburn. Vol. XXXV. New York, 1908.

————. *Fiction Fair and Foul*. In *The Works of John Ruskin*, ed. E. T. Cook and Alexander Wedderburn. Vol. XXXIV. New York, 1908.

Rutherford, Andrew. *Byron: A Critical Study*. London, 1961.

Saintsbury, George. *A History of English Prosody from the Twelfth Century to the Present Day*. Vol. III. New York, 1961.

BIBLIOGRAPHY

Santayana, George. *Scepticism and Animal Faith: Introduction to a System of Philosophy*. New York, 1923.

Schiff, Hermann. *Über Lord Byrons 'Marino Faliero' und seine anderen geschichtlichen Dramen*. Marburg, 1910.

Shelley, Percy Bysshe. *Complete Poetical Works*, ed. Thomas Hutchinson, with intro. and notes by B. P. Kurtz. New York, 1933.

Smith, Charles J. "The Contrarieties: Wordsworth's Dualistic Imagery." *PMLA*, LXIX (1954), 1181-1199.

Smith, Horatio and James. *Rejected Addresses: or, the new Theatrum poetarum*. 3rd American edn. Boston, 1841.

Spacks, Patricia Meyer. "'Artful Strife': Conflict in Gray's Poetry." *PMLA*, LXXXI (1966), 63-69.

Stapfer, Paul. *Montaigne*. Paris, 1895.

Stavrou, C. N. "Religion in Byron's *Don Juan*." *SEL*, III (1963), 567-594.

Steffan, Truman Guy, and Willis W. Pratt. *Byron's Don Juan*. 4 vols. Austin, Texas, 1957.

Stevens, Wallace. *Notes toward a Supreme Fiction*. Cummington, Massachusetts, 1942.

————. *Collected Poems*. New York, 1954.

Swedenberg, H. T. *The Theory of the Epic in England: 1650-1800*. Berkeley and Los Angeles, 1944.

Tave, Stuart M. *The Amiable Humorist: A Study in the Comic Theory of the Eighteenth and Early Nineteenth Centuries*. Chicago, 1960.

Thorslev, Peter Larsen. *The Byronic Hero: Types and Prototypes*. Minneapolis, Minnesota, 1962.

————. "Freedom and Destiny: Romantic Contraries." *Bucknell Review*, XIV (May 1966), 38-45.

Trueblood, Paul Graham. *The Flowering of Byron's Genius; Studies in Byron's Don Juan*. Palo Alto, Calif., 1945.

Ullmann, Stephen de. "Romanticism and Synaesthesia: A Comparative Study of Sense Transfer in Keats and Byron." *PMLA*, LX (1945), 811-827.

Van Doren, Mark. *John Dryden: A Study of His Poetry*. 3rd edn. New York, 1946.

Van Rennes, J. J. *Byron, Bowles, and the Pope Controversy*. Amsterdam, 1927.

Vivante, Leone. *English Poetry and its Contribution to the Knowledge of a Creative Principle*. New York, 1950.

Wasserman, Earl R. *The Subtler Language: Critical Readings of Neoclassical and Romantic Poems*. Baltimore, Maryland, 1959.

————. "The English Romantics: The Grounds of Knowledge." *SiR*, IV (1964), 17-34.

West, Paul, ed. *Byron: A Collection of Critical Essays*. New Jersey, 1963.

Wilkie, Brian. *Romantic Poets and Epic Tradition*. Madison and Milwaukee, Wisconsin, 1965.

Willey, Basil. *The Seventeenth Century Background*. New York, 1950.

[Wilson, John.] "Childe Harold's Pilgrimage: Canto the Fourth." *Edinburgh Review*, xxx (1818), 87-120.

Wordsworth, William. *Poetical Works*, with intro. and notes, ed. Thomas Hutchinson. New edn., rev. by Ernest de Selincourt. London, 1959.

―――. *The Prelude; or Growth of a Poet's Mind*, ed. from the mss. with intro., textual and critical notes by Ernest de Selincourt. 2nd edn., rev. by Helen Darbishire. Oxford, 1959.

―――. *The Prose Works. For the first time collected, with additions from unpublished mss.* ed., with preface, notes and illustrations, by Alexander B. Grosart. London, 1876.

―――. *Wordsworth's Literary Criticism*, ed. with an intro. by Nowell C. Smith. London, 1905.

INDEX

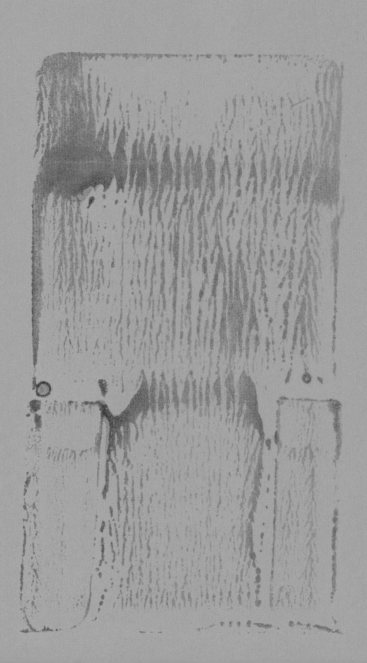